Time is Ticking
The Fifth Amendment

Vie Loriot de Rouvray

Independently Published by: VIE Loriot de Rouvray
www.authorvie.com

ISBN: 979-8-9897845-7-8
ISBN: 979-8-9897845-8-5

DEDICATION

"I dedicate this book to the Holy Spirit, His Energy, and Power"

VIE

Table of Contents

Prologue

As a French/American Author, I feel guided to remind everyone today of some of the facts about The Statue of Liberty. She stands at the entrance of New York Harbor, a 151-foot statue of a woman holding a book and a torch on high.

"Liberty Enlightening the World" was a gift from the people of France to the United States as a symbol of Friendship, Freedom, and Peace between the US and France.

The statue is of a robed female figure representing Libertas, the Roman goddess of freedom, who bears a torch and a tabula ansata (a tablet evoking the law).

The world has become crazy. Craving for Power through destruction, genocide, wars, and Money.

Life is about Friendship, Sharing, Love, Compassion, Freedom, and Peace.

Death is about graduation, the Soul has no color and never dies but only graduates or fails, Hell...! Money is the root of every evil; therefore, money should never be worshiped in guiding you.

Let us continue to stand united together and create a New World of friendship, Freedom, Love, and Peace. A word about Oligarchy.

Oligarchy is a form of government in which all power is vested in a few number of persons or a dominant class or "clique" government by the few. They're what you get in a "religious" oligarchy, which is trying to sustain their special privilege against the tides of change.

Negative multidimensional beings in key places play a part in the exercise of power in the shadow of human oligarchy, a form of power structure in which power effectively rests with a small number of people.

The straightest path to the truth is to expose all information that is officially forbidden.

Once you remember your multidimensionality then Christ will awaken in you. It is Time!

WHO ARE THE PLEIADIAN

Who are the Pleiadians Emissaries of Light, and why do they want to help us, why do they care about us living our soul's purpose?

The Pleiadians are lovers and truth givers, and they seek only to be of service, and they are back here for that purpose. To help you create a world of FREEDOM, Compassion, and Peace where love will reign supreme.

The Pleiadians Emissaries of Light are Star friends who have been watching over us for many years. They are from the star system Pleiades, yet they traverse many universes. The state of humanity reflects not only their Universe but many others. May you all be blessed by your infinite Light!

Synopsis

"The many layers of Gauze"

In Search on the VADJRA...The KEY to the Universe

VIE and CHADD begin their search for the VAJRA that was taken by an Asian couple from VIE when she was intoxicated. The VAJRA has been sent somewhere to be part of an ancient pagan ritual on a solstice.

The eternally warring factions (a small, organized, dissenting group within a larger one) of the Cathari are exposed to the world. The VAJRA is recovered by only the Divine intervention of God and his followers.

One day VIE's life changed after the reunion with her blue flame. She entered a world of conspiracy and lies for eight years but more was to come. To set you free the Fifth Amendment breach has been discovered and is exposed.

"This afternoon I was on a mission; I was not simply here to enjoy a cup of coffee and a good reading. I knew I was here to meet, him, someone that would change my entire life.

I heard a voice… It stirred a passion deep within me.

Yes, a yearning began from the innermost vessels of my heart.

The voice spoke…" What do you do...?"… but the question was far deeper - he was asking for much more than that. I knew He was asking for my assistance, my strength, my well of living waters.

I have been trained in the mysteries of the Cosmic Mother in Egypt and guided by Archangel Michael. Through movements, Light, and sounds inner doors opened and freed me again and I began to appreciate my long-time gifts and their challenges.

For, I had been trained in the temples of Isis to the art of using my powers ... I was able to direct those healing powers to transform the hearts of men... and I knew this man, and He was asking me for my troth, my heart, and my sustaining strength.

He knew he had still much to face in the coming times and he would need my quiet source of power and strength again.

The Energetic Power of the Feminine Essence and I also gave him my heart. We know have a connection at the heart center." Failure is not an option. When the two Sacred Fires, God's Pink Flame of Divine Love and our Father God's Blue Flame of Divine Power, merge into higher frequencies of the 7th Solar Aspect of Deity, which is the 5th-dimensional Crystalline Solar Violet Flame. The glorious Violet Flame is the predominant influence on Earth during the 2,000-year cycle of the Aquarian Age we are now entering.

"I Am the chosen one Marie-Madeleine. I Am come to infuse the Divine Feminine upon the Earth and I Am that same Marie-Madeleine who was with Jesus of Nazareth when He walked the Earth Plane. I Am married to him. I Am his other half.

I Am come to do the same blessed work now, as I did then. Vibration Intuitive Energy: The Light has come with the Sound; Love leads the way now.

I Am sent from Heaven's Realm to bring You a message.

I encourage You to shine from Your Heart Space from the Divine Omniscient I am Presence of All That Is commonly known as "The Source" for many are being caught up in world auric fields that cause fear, nervousness, and stress (from third energy vortex).

Therefore, it is for You to stand in Your Heart Space and stay in balance through the great Love coming from Heaven's Realm infused into these beautiful Lunar and Light Rays, straight to Your illumined heart chamber which links You directly with us.

I Bless You with the Love and Blessings of Those of Heaven's Realm who have sent Me. The Highest of The Highest. Great I Am Omniscient Presence …Dare to be who you are, you, you are beautiful! The Christ energy awakens in all of you. Feel the presence of Christ in your inner space. The feeling is Love for you.

Christ demonstrated alchemy with his blood by taking the fermented grape and changing it into his blood.

Blessed Be, Blessed Be.

In Love and Light always,

Summary

Saint Michael The Archangel

It was in early fall, and I was driving my car towards the Institute office. I had an appointment very early that day. I normally avoid early appointments as it takes me about an hour to prepare the office room and myself before any client.

When suddenly Archangel Michael was sitting on the passenger seat next to me.

Archangel Michael began to talk to me.

"VIE how are you doing today? We have some work to do together. You have been chosen to be the door to the Divine. Then began a long work of twelve hours a day for the following eighteen months from which I do not recall many details. Then I was guided to do some very spiritual work and some research and to read a lot about medicine and health. To study all that was about health and drugs and its effects all over the world and on the world in different cultures and places.

I began to awaken. My memory began to return. My life with him that I share since many lives, our work together, Why I have been chosen, and why I am now working directly and only under the creator.

I came back with something so unique, so different and so powerful to share with humanity and I found that all human beings are under the control of negative multidimensional beings forces. I now have to battle to help the planet out of this control to be able to acknowledge my work and find me to receive what I have come to share with them. DNA has been reduced to a few strands, subliminal is used to keep their brain where it shouldn't be, the trap of drugs, the mental facilities to brainwash and keep people as puppets, the manipulation of the brain to commit crimes, and other horrific acts, people in sleepwalking enslaved. And to guide my blue flame...

And I have to "manage this mess" as he kept saying to find our way together.

All his life he had to fight for his life. Even his brain has been programmed. Katherine, stood by his bedside many, many times while he was sleeping and whispered evil words in his ears, then during a coma, he was programmed through evil hard rock tones of music, and then he was bombarded while in mental hospitals by specific TV series forced to look at by his Government imposed "Mentor". A man who by choice turned himself at a very young age to the dark forces and made slowly his way up and influential in key places in the system.

Military, Civil, legal, and political.

I am now fighting the entire system by myself while they control my blue flame, CHADD, through "justice" and the Court with drugs, shots of drugs, beating, poisoning, asylum, mental hospitalizations, and Katrine's manipulation of his brain.

They handicapped him through unnecessary surgery, depriving him of sleep, rights, and freedom, and used him for their movie projects. They use him as a musician, stunt, security agent, FBI, and much more without any compensation.

But what they did not expect was the Father to send me with all his power to help him. To be here to witness, report, and, to you the truth of fact and reality.

Definitions

CHADD: Tainted Angel.

VIE: Door to the Divine and the chosen one.

DARK GOVERNMENT: The Secret Government. Dark energies that elected themselves in Key power places in the Government. Goes by code names.

ILLUMINATI: Secret Government

ARCHONS/JENS: Reptilian bloodlines

VAJRA: Key to the Universe given to VIE by a Tibetan Master. The mighty me "a bolt of lightning" transmission of blessing helps to heal the etheric field, which is God.

ANKH: means VIE (life). Union of heaven and earth. Oneness.

WAKOVA: Jesus

WANEKA: Messiah

CARLOS: Beat CHADD under camera

RONALD: Astrologist

KATHERINE: CHADD step-mom, archon reptilian bloodlines

NATACHA: Nurse

LEE MINH: Chinese nurse, hate VIE

BAKITINN: High authorities in Court

FORREST: Judge

CAROLINA: Social Worker

PAUL: CHADD half-brother

JORGE GRICE: Imposed CHADD mentor

AMELIE: Sent to VIE by Government

MAMA CLAMBI: Indonesian cook

KASSAN: Indonesian handy-man

NETTE: Sister

NANOUNE: Sister

LICOU: Sister

THUGGEE: Re-incarnated Killers Indian Dark forces.

MITSY: Dealer-ship employee

PATRICIA: VIE friend

PASTOR DARKIN: Works for secret Government at I-V convert church

Dr. MINGH: A doctor in charge at IBEHAVE mental hospital

Dr. GANAKJAM: Doctor in IBEHAVE

Dr. KASHIN: Pakistani, she works at the Walking Center

DR. SINGHAM: Los Angeles doctor

DR. VANGALI: Sand Diego doctor

Dr. GANDAM: San Francisco doctor

Dr KAOS: Backerinim Asylum

Dr. HERNANDEZ: Backerinim

ANTOINETTE: Haitian cleaning woman

AFFIA & ASSIM KALSAM: Owns IBEHAVE mental Hospital and the Psychiatric Regional Center

BETSY: Works for the Regional Psychiatric office

PASTOR DAVIS: Minister at United Church

FATHER RAVI: Priest

KISHORE: Indian police officer

BRANDY: Defense attorney and cousin

McCONRAID: 1rst M.D. that has put CHADD in Psychiatric drugs at 5 years old

PAOLITO: gifted healer

MARIA TRANH-KRUGER: recovered the VAJRA.

INTRODUCTION

This book follows the first part and book titled "Destiny of the doG". This is where it all makes sense.

I have been chosen to be the door to the Divine. I lived many lives before this one, but I came back to help you, and to accomplish a mission that is to help you become your own master. To recover the freedom that has been given to you by God.

My blue flame came back to me, and He is the catalyst for this book.

This book is dedicated to the Holy Spirit, bringing powerful messages to the world. With warnings and future predictions that you may not want to hear.
It is about hope, courage, and freedom.

Prophecies fulfilled

A battle of evil and good.

The matrix and the ascension process.

My name is VIE, I am your guide into the light and the darkness as I remember them. I can raise your vibration and reconnect your DNA through different ways of using my Light energy. Using the sound frequency of my voice and the language of the Light or by sending you energy from my heart center. Your reconnection to the Quantum matrix is essential. I came to awaken new frequencies within One's being and help humanity embrace the Light and Sound of creation to expand consciousness. It then aligns you to your path in awakening its memory by unlocking the program.

Our purpose is to defragment old programming that no longer serves you and to replace it with the Light and Sound frequencies of the Divine plan. Space, will then, be created to incorporate new harmonies in the body of the human, and through this, healing on all plans occurs.

Powerfully transformational words and tones facilitate a return to who you are with accelerated healing, removal of blocks, DNA recoding, emotional re-patterning, and Light codes, frequencies, and activations for your ascension. I am the first Aquarius to come with a knowledge that will take humanity a little more than 2,000 years to integrate.

I was led to remember who I was on the other side of the veil, for what purpose, and what gifts I was coming back on earth with. Also, to reconnect with my blue flame and husband of a long-time CHADD with whom we were already working together for humanity for eons, in Egypt, and Atlantis.

I came here, to this planet Earth with an appropriate body for living in this 3D (third dimension) reality. I was born at a certain moment with the astrological chart that I chose and was guided to have for that mission.

When the Secret Government and the Thuggees found me, my work, and my office all my troubles began. They followed me, intoxicated me, sent me to jail, vandalized the institute office, contacted my family, and fed them false information hoping that they would baker-act me and institutionalize me, they infiltrated a social worker as a client and other clients to get information, they made my work and office invisible to the public to bankrupt me. They tried to buy my Lawyer... They nearly killed my blue flame. With broken pieces of glass in his food, arsenic in his water, chemical drops in his food while he was maintained in a mental facility, injection of drugs he was allergic to, dropped him out of his wheelchair and beat him, tried to break his arm and access to his brain inserting a pen in his ear while he was sleeping still in the same mental and hospital owned by thugees.

But they still did not figure out why I did not give up.

Maybe that is the difference between an Angel of God and fallen Angels (Reptilians, archons, secret Government, Third world order) I have peace and they don't.

"I Am the chosen one, Marie-Madeleine. I have come to infuse the Divine Feminine upon the Earth and I Am that same Marie-Madeleine who was with Jesus of Nazareth when he walked the Earth Plane. I Am married to him. I Am his other half.

I have come to do the same blessed work now, as I did then. Vibration Intuitive Energy: The Light has come with the Sound; Love leads the way now.

I Am sent from Heaven's Realm to bring You a message.

"I encouraged You to shine from Your Heart Space from the Divine Omniscient. I am the Presence of All That Is commonly known as 'The Source" for many are being caught up in world auric fields that cause fear, nervousness, and stress (from the third energy vortex) Therefore, it is for You to stand in Your Heart Space and stay in balance through the great Love coming from Heaven's Realm, straight to Your illumined heart chamber which links You directly with us.

I Bless You with the Love and Blessings of Those of Heaven's Realm who have sent Me. The Highest of The Highest. Great I Am Omniscient Presence …Dare to be who you are, you are beautiful! The Christ energy awakens in all of you. Feel the presence of Christ in your inner space. Feel his Love for you."

Christ demonstrated alchemy with his blood by taking the fermented grape and changing it into his blood.

One day Mother Mary said to her son: "My Lord, I have heard that the prophets have entered into the Light. And Christ answered her that no prophet has entered into the Light, but the archons of the aeons have spoken with them from the aeons and have given them the mystery of aeons, and when He came to the regions of the aeons, He turned Elijah into the body of John the baptizer, and the others that he turned around, directing them into the righteous bodies that will find the mysteries of the Light, ascend on high, and inherit the Light-kingdom"

Christ Jesus makes it clear that there are many levels of ascension, but to go beyond existence in the son of the universe requires Christ to open the thresholds which were shut to the higher Light realms since the fall of Lucifer, Adam, and "Sophia". Christ has also reset the course of the aeons so that they will now have the opportunity to involve in the regions of the right and the higher dimensional worlds of the Treasury of Light. Christ also said "As Abraham and

Isaac and Jacob, I have forgiven all their sins and their transgressions and have given them the mysteries of the Light in the aeons and stationed them in the regions of the sealer of the seven force fields and of all the archons who have repented. And when I go to the Height and I am ready to go into the Light, I will take their souls with me into the Light, but amen I say to you, Mary: They will not enter into the Light before I have taken your soul and all those of your brothers into the Light."

Christian theology after the council of Nicea (325 C.E.) officially rejected the concept and doctrine of reincarnation. But in the earlier Coptic Christians (Egyptian) and the Near-Eastern texts (related to the Old Testament) Christ never closed the door to the reappearance of the Ancient Testament saints prophets that were blessed through Divine Grace to bring forth a participatory message of the Truth, for many higher souls that wanted to come back and help. Christ manifested at zero point in history to evolve humanity into empathy which is the highest point of the Age of Pisces. Empathy opens humans to spiritual access, and Christ came as a model of the nine-dimensional human. Which is what all of you will become during the Age of Aquarius. Christ came and brought what can transmute human violence "the Eucharist", to activate the plant Gaia's habitat.

Christ did that after he inseminated me, He delivered his bloodline through me. He planted his star codes in my physical body. Christ brought Gaian alchemy by transmitting plants into blood; his blood flows in your veins and this is your antidote to mind control. The world management dark forces team diverted you from this knowledge by getting you all to obsess about addictions, so you have forgotten the plant power, the sun in the grapes. You bought into the idea that everything is negative on your planet, and you lost your ability to focus on how you are using things in your reality. Then you lost access to the "chaotic plants" the most potent activators of the etheric. Romans expected Niburu to become the chosen people who would arrive. The Eucharist was swallowed hook, line, and sinker, and it became the main ritual of the Roman Catholic Church for the Age of Pisces. The Romans decided to use it as fuel for converting the world and to take control they first wiped Marie-Madeleine out of the records. Later, once they murdered the Cathars, all priests were to be celibate to make people eventually believe that Christ was celibate. This would eliminate the potential discovery of the bloodline because, even if the DNA survived, nobody would believe it was real.

This ceremony was invented first by a Sirian/pagan, it was possible to keep all nine dimensions open for 2000 years. The early medieval works of Hildegard Von Bingen like Thomas Aquinas reflect the power of this vibration before the Roman Catholic Church chose the net instead of the Web of Light. By stealing the alchemical transubstantiation of Christ, the Roman Catholic Church created a Meltdown. This time is over.

I Bless You with the Love and Blessings of Those of Heaven's Realm who have sent Me. The Highest of The Highest. Great I Am Omniscient Presence ...

My life as VIE looks like it has been divided into five phases I was born on a tiny little Island living on a big private property facing the most beautiful beaches of the capital. Only friends and employees were part of our life as we had no neighbors around and there was no road access to the public. My Mother never cooked never went grocery shopping or had to clean the house. She was our father's Queen. She never worked and never had to worry about making a check or paying a bill. She just had to enjoy life and travel with him for business purposes. Mother was very strict when we were young but then became a sweet unconditionally loving person. Love that we received plenty and as much as we needed. She lived for her husband and through her father. She was found and deeply in love with him. They must have had some arguments at some point, like every couple but we never heard or were aware of it.

My father was a rich industrial and great businessman. Many would consult him. He was very busy with his business but when he was home, he had always time to take care of us. Its great pride was to be seen with us in public. We never heard the word money. Money subject was not allowed.

We had an Indonesian woman surnamed Mama Clambi. Our father recruited her after paying her debts at playing cards and from that day on she considered herself as part of the family and us as her children. She was very devoted to our family. She was a wonderful Indonesian and exotic cook and learned very quickly to cook French cuisine too. But we liked better her exotic food, and we would often sneak into her house to eat some Indonesian food that she cooked for her and Palidjo.

Kassan was the Indonesian house's handyman; House cleaning and lawn guy and he was babysitting when needed. A very gentle and calm person. One day when Kassan was sick my sister Chris who was very young, five or six at that time, gave him some tea. He never forgot and since that day he called her Nette, and he became very protective of her.

My older sister has always been very independent and the preferred one of my aunt Tiphaine whom we familiarly called our second mother.

I was the second daughter and I have always been called the "different one" of the family.
The third of us called Nanoune by our cook would have never lived without her loving care and patience. That is what my Mother has always affirmed. She was never hungry. The Cook, her nanny, had to swing her under the Banyan tree, and would for hours keep trying to have a swallow one spoon or a bite at a time every half an hour or so when she was lucky. Nanoune would say repetitively when refusing the spoon" Mama Clambi the food is cold" and Mama Clambi would go and heat the food. Then she would say" Mama Clambi it's hot" and her nanny would wait and try again when it was not so hot.

My youngest sister was a very easy little girl and baby. She was always happy. She had her nanny two named Nana. And she learned to speak Indonesian. She had long curled hair and did not like her nanny to comb it. She thought it was too painful, but her nanny had to do it and she would say "Addoo Nana" meaning it is hurting me, Nana...

Our life was run by school and family enjoying the beach with some invited friends.

Later on, getting older our teenage friends were always welcomed home and at our table.

Our father offered me my first car, and our great friend Alain and his brothers and sister had a beautiful sailing boat. Life was easy and I began to enjoy sailing to islands for picnics. It was current that Alain's little brother named Minette would enter our house by an open window and we would find him sleeping in one of our beds.

I was entering my third life chapter when my best friend Jacquie convinced me, one day, to apply with her to work for the same company. We wanted to travel and see the world. It was quite common to stay between Flights as long as five to seven days in an all-paid 5-star hotel. We always had a very busy time shopping and visiting, learning about the different cultures and their life.

With my fourth life episode, I began my Spiritual Journey. I met many interesting, unexpected, and different people from all types of backgrounds and good friends when I traveled to Central America. I heard about a few shamans, and I began to have many visions...

My dreams made me remember a lot from the island when growing up. I remembered one man who was in his forties and who from one day to another regressed crawling on the floor. He dated a woman from a tribe. They poisoned him and the man never recovered. I have seen some mining lab tests turning like crazy in the testing glass without reason that would not be stabilized, so the chemist could not read the results. Due to some witchcraft coming from a competitor...

But I have also learned to read and predict the weather on the island. I have also learned since then that predicting the wind was not something that applied automatically everywhere. I have been taught to avoid swimming at a specific time when the shark would come closer to the beach just by looking at the ski.

This fourth life episode of my life lasted around five years and preceded "Nine Years of Dark Novena"
Then suddenly talking to my friend Ron and I heard myself telling him, this chapter is closed now I can go forward. I could feel it strongly.

Edward (CHADD's father) whose health was declining had a heart attack and died. Katerine was struck by a ball of white light, and nothing was left of her body to be found. But later she will send a Gypsy dark energy ghost to control, limit, hurt, and dominate CHADD. But not for long. As soon as VIE discovered it she sent it right back to where it came from.

CHADD at the same time saw the Ruby placed on the roof that was guiding him in the dark to VIE.

The keeper of the Sacred Knowledge resides on the planet. It is the sweet perfume of freedom that incites you to recall your reconnection to the source.

But the VAJRA, the key to the Universe that has been taken away from VIE when CHADD and VIE were intoxicated and arrested has been sent to be part of an ancient pagan ritual on a Solstice to celebrate a Greek goddess.

A Greek underworld goddess representing night and darkness associated with sorcery, the black arts deception at the inter-dimensional crossroads. Instead of the seventy-two Divine names of the Godhead she carries seventy-seven demonic entities whose purpose is to destroy humanity. It is how the Cathars were destroyed by Rome, by these Archons and their knowledge. They manipulated forces outside of human form. All archons are the goddess Devil's forces.

They control the population through false and withheld information and are in key power places. Courts, judges, lawyers, Psychologists Doctors, mental behavioral facilities and mental Hospitals, Pharmaceutical companies, Churches and religious personalities, policemen, sheriffs, politicians, press and TVs, and behind the cameras. Their agenda is to reduce the population and to manipulate humanity keeping them under their control through drugs, flu and antibiotic shots, implanted diseases, weather catastrophes, and wars.

This demoniac goddess Hekate is the third order that has blocked the power of the true Trinity with its triple-faced and its twenty-seven arch-demons under her command. The archdemons entered humanity and brought them to falsehoods and lies. The souls stolen by her are turned over to her demons under her control, so that they may torment them until destruction.

The Angels' Cosmic couple, CHADD & VIE, returned at this crucial time on earth, at a time when political corruption and financial instability with global religious tensions are at summon. The earth is in chaos.

Humans are beginning to awaken and trying to find their purpose, with the Ebola resurfacing. Autism has never been so high in numbers. The opening of the third eye is important but has been calcified and beings have been disconnected from the heart to be kept in fear. Pharmaceutical companies are flourishing, Psychiatry is booming and mental hospitals like evaluation centers are fully booked. Asylums cover up dead people inside their places. People die mysteriously in Hospitals...

But most of the population has not been prepared for the truth they have been misled by lies and false information. They do not understand what battles lie under.

They have been kept unaware of the underlying of the Ascension.

Time has never been so crucial and CHADD & VIE, have to go through many more tribulations to free humanity and recover the VAJRA before the solstice.

They are battling the enemies without ceasing to go through attempted murders. CHADD is more than ever arrested and admitted and trapped in the IBEHAVE hospital, where he is battling the third and fourth orders. VIE is his protection and only outside link but ordered not to communicate with him.

Many ascended Masters are walking back to Earth. Saints, Angels Archangels, guides, and protectors are helping during this important time of ascension, but also satanic energies like the Thuggees.

Many souls are leaving the planet, their contract accomplished or murdered by dark Souls that are also reincarnated on Earth.

The "Illuminati team" is trying hard to kill CHADD.

Chapter 1
A European Reporter, A Scoop, and an International Law Suit

When the black Government authorities in power understood what we were here for and that we were sent by the Father, they used all their power to separate us and kill CHADD. They sent CHADD to an asylum (a concentration camp) for nearly 2 years. In this asylum they kill people, cover it up, and bury them in the location. And nobody will ever hear from them again.

Every day the guardians let CHADD out of his concrete cage, which was so small that his wheelchair would not fit, and no one could stand up inside, so he was seated and sleeping on the concrete floor, it was humid, and he had no blanket. He was out of his concrete cage each day for fifteen minutes in cool air and his guardians would incessantly tell him next week or by tomorrow or in two days... you will move up. Which never happened until he was released.

He was released and sent straight back to jail in his town "house", then to court where they sentenced him to twelve months in a halfway house, with no guards or surveillance on the location where dangerous murderers and criminals live.

He had no phone and was cut off from all outside communication.

During his first night, the bed he was sleeping on broke, and CHADD fell on the floor and hurt himself badly. He kept calling for help in pain, but no one came. After many attempts in the early morning, he finally could get back up in his wheelchair, in excruciating pain, and rolled himself out in the street. He was hungry and thirsty. The night before he opened the refrigerator to get food and a large male living in the same half-house covered with tattoos everywhere on his body, full of marks left from fights by knives and gunshots appeared next to him and closed the refrigerator saying: "You don't touch this food, this is mine!"

So, CHADD was now in the street in a wheelchair when he saw a Christian prayer on the door of one house. He rolled to the front and knocked at the door. A friendly man with a strong Latin accent asked him what he could do for him and gave him many sandwiches and drinks. CHADD told him everything and the friendly man called the ambulance as CHADD was in pain and hurt from his fall from bed. CHADD was transported to the nearest emergency room for treatment and called me for help.

VIE hired a European reporter and a lawsuit at the International Court in Hagues was issued for genocides and crimes against humanity using medical institutions:

"Governmental and medical institutions code menaces to authority as mental diseases during political disturbances."

Nowadays political prisoners in states, and around the Globe, are sometimes confined and abused in mental institutions, and psychiatric confinement of sane people is a particularly pernicious form of repression used by the secret Government.

Psychiatry possesses a built-in capacity for abuse that is greater than in other areas of medicine. The diagnosis of mental disease allows the state to hold persons against their will and insist upon therapy in their interest and the broader interests of society. In addition, receiving a psychiatric diagnosis can in itself be regarded as oppressive.

Psychiatry is used to bypass standard legal procedures for establishing guilt or innocence and allow political incarceration without the ordinary odium attached to such political trials. "A breach of the constitution in the states and a violation of the fifth amendment."

Now it is expanding to families with disharmony at home and it extends to extortion of money. Parents and families are backers acting their family members to get "better" through false advertisements and fake promises. Parents who are aware of the potential danger of autism due to vaccinations and who refuse to have their children vaccinated, or poisoned by pharmaceutical drugs, are susceptible to imprisonment.

The use of hospitals instead of jails prevents the victims from receiving legal aid before the courts makes indefinite incarceration possible and discredits the individuals and their ideas. In that manner, whenever open trials are desirable, they are avoided.

CHADD is a perfect example after years and years kept as their guinea pig. He has been brutalized many times. Once, in the middle of his sleep inside the facility, someone tried to force a pen into his ears to get into his brain. He has been deprived of nutrients, forced to drink tap water with chlorine, then after got sick by ingesting too much juice trying to rehydrate his body.

They attempted to kill him several times in many ways. He was pulled out of his wheelchair, dragged under a cold shower, stripped out of his clothes, dumped on the floor and his skull beaten on the shower floor to finally be punched in his face by a gigantic male nurse, while he could not reach for his chair.

CHADD received shot injections, and pills, that his body is allergic to, though it was noted in his file. It's been going on for so long, so many years, so many different drugs that he already had a stroke, but they still gave him the same pills to swallow. He has now been diagnosed with a heart problem and the pills make him very depressed with suicidal thoughts. All hospitals, institutions, and the asylum he is admitted and locked into are not built for wheelchairs or the handicapped. When a wheelchair passes the doors, it hurts his fingers and often they split open to bleeding and scaring. Showers are not adapted either and become an adventure, using the bathrooms is hell and every day is a life and death combat.

Chapter 2
Ron Gets Attacked Again By Invisible Forces

I told Ron this chapter was closed now, and I could move forward, and the following day Ron called me.

"VIE last night after we decided in our meeting to discuss what you told me in more detail, I began to feel very sick. I was attacked by an invisible force that tried to strangle me then by placing invisible insects all over my body. I can still see the bites. It was so strong that I was bleeding all over and I had to jump in the shower. Now I cannot walk, half of my face is distorted, and I am in such a pain that I cannot even brush my teeth nor touch them. I am in agonizing pain."

I went to consult my acupuncture friend and he does not understand what is happening to me. He saw the scars and the bleeding but could not find anything else to help me although my body was hot then turned cold and the pain was there.

This is the third time in one year that I was attacked when I went to meet with you. Last month I was just mentioning your name to our Friends Tahnee and Bob, since all my business went down to the point where I was very close to considering living in my car. I could barely pay my rent.

Today I am sick, attacked by invisible energies and so in pain that I have to stay in bed, and I cannot schedule anybody. I am very concerned and wondering how I will be able to pay my rent and if I am still sick, I do not see myself sleeping in a car.

My computer is not working, my printer prints by itself, my paintings and all my art have fallen off the wall and I have no explanation whatsoever. It is obvious that meeting with you is disturbing someone with dark energy."

But who else that Katherine, Carlos, Paul, and Carolina can be? And Why?

Chapter 3
The Encounter with a Medium Whale

I entered the waiting room and did not see anyone in but then I heard "Here you are!"

VIE: How did you know?

Him: "I am a medium."

I proceeded to the counter and heard "VIE", do not leave without me. I want you to meet someone. He is waiting for me downstairs.

I hurried to the counter and headed back to the door exit, and he followed me to the elevator.

We came out of the building, and I followed him to the parking lot where a man was sitting in the driver's seat.

"VIE, meet my friend the rain forest man, and let's follow each other and have a coffee at Whole Foods as we are not far from it." I was intrigued and very excited simultaneously. I wanted to hear more about these two men.

He was careful of our surroundings and very cautious of all he was saying and finally in a very low tone said.

"Look we are a Spiritual family. No one must know I am here. They are killing all the whales. They trap them. I am one of them. You have to help. I will teach you the tone. They must hide. I will be going back home with them soon. I was in Indonesia, I worked with the children, and they were very receptive. But the enemy found me. They took over my work, my company, and my children. Luckily, I found the rainforest man. He knows we will not be able to be roommates anymore soon. But I still have a little time and another mission before. I am leaving for Thailand very soon. I must go and help the poor women to deliver, they cannot pay, and I have to teach math to the children. They understand and are very receptive.

I met him one more time. He taught me the warning and reunion song for the whales and vanished. I never heard of them again.

But I have been able to put all the children that came in session with me, then after, to communicate with whales and to communicate with their energy and the energy of nature.

Until the secret Government found me and my work, and from that day on the trouble with my work began. They tried first to intimidate me by vandalizing the office, destroying my computer, having helicopters flying over my house, and destroying two of my laptops. They hijacked my websites many times and made me invisible to the public.

It's been nine years of fight. Nine years of expenses with monthly rent and advertisements... without any return. They are waiting for me to bankrupt like vultures, while CHADD is fighting the demons for his health and his life.

Chapter 4
Sternum Broken

The tribulations continue.

I, VIE, dropped him at Carlos' house that evening, and I received a weird phone call around midnight.

It was nearly incomprehensible. Both were talking at the same time and the phone was breaking up with a lot of background confusing noises.

Carlos' voice finally came louder and clearer and he told me "We were at the Riviera resort bar he fell from his chair, has bruises, and has chest pain. He wants you to meet us at the Hospital Emergency Room."

CHADD had left me a copy of his driver's license, as Mitsy from the Car eternity dealership did not give him back his driver's license, and he had no papers to present at the emergency room.

I was far from expecting what I saw and hearing the explanation of what happened. His arms were all bruised and violet. His head was painful, he was having chest pains, and his eyes were all red. The X-rays came back positive his sternum was broken.

In reality, he had been pulled out of Carlos' car passenger seat and beaten by 12 guys, and it all happened under a camera.

Carlos, a man from the secret Government, had his exotic ex-girlfriend, tattoo CHADD's name and Carlos wanted CHADD to "marry" the girl.

Of course, CHADD refused, and Carlos called his friends to come and join to beat him up. He was not only beaten up but also, they pulled a gun on him. Security finally came but he was already all bruised.

This was a cover-up version. CHADD was once again used for a movie; he saw how the car backed up on him to ensure that the scene was under at least one of the cameras.

So, from midnight till 8 am, I was at the emergency room waiting for the results to know if CHADD would be released.

We left had a coffee, and a croissant then went to meet our friend Arnold.

Ten days later and early evening CHADD decided to visit his friend Johnny hoping to be able to sleep over at his place.

Around 3 pm that afternoon, CHADD called me.

He went to meet with Carolina, an empowered woman, court-appointed, who owns a rehabilitation facility called "Ibehave" and an assisted living facility, he gave the woman, in cash, the complete amount of his monthly disability check, as every month and Carlos drove him into the "Ibehave" center to be admitted. Why?

They took all his personal belongings, his golden chain and cross his ring, iPhone as collateral when he was admitted. But collateral for what?

Chapter 5
Typhon the Third Archon

Suddenly, I realized that I have to take time to slow down, reflect, and take more time for myself.

There is a time of pain, there is a time of sadness like there were and like they are, and times of joy and happiness. And I am tired, so tired. No one seems to understand.

Many worships but an ideal. I am so sad and so tired.

There is religion, which is largely about arguing over which ancient beliefs about God are correct and getting others to believe the same things you believe. They all fight for the best denominations or religions. But how many know him? How many are close to him, I think?

Then I heard my Angels saying.

"You are right, VIE not many people. Many people in the entertainment industry have been hired by the government to distract the masses by making human beings happy and docile so that people don't know what's going on. They decide these things out in the woods in a circle, at night, and naked.

Freemasonry and Protestantism have a link. Freemasonry has been created by two protestant pastors and Mormons religion has been created by the free-masons.

Every year a group of men involved with high levels of politics and finance meet in secrecy in a remote area of California. These families have ties to practically every industry that exists today, including Hollywood. The origins of these families are also connected to esoteric occult organizations, such as Freemasonry. This is where occult symbolism, such as the triangle and all-seeing Eye comes into fruition. The theory states that many Hollywood hopefuls display these symbols, which are hidden in plain sight, to show their allegiance to the 'global elite' and to better themselves within the industry.

Illuminati is the hidden governing force (secret Government) that has ties in all of today's biggest industries, including financial, entertainment, military, and religious. Illuminati references have become ubiquitous throughout Hollywood, as seen in several films, television shows, music videos, and even live performances and CHADD mentor is one of them.

It is a sunny day; I am worrying as it's been days now since I heard from my blue flame. I am trying to keep myself occupied. I decided to call my friend Patricia and see if we could have lunch together. I am out of the shower and finishing to dress when finally, the phone is ringing. I am so happy to hear from him but not for long. His voice is very low, and he is talking very fast.

CHADD to me "The Father visited me last night. I knew something big was going to come. I went to visit the paradise. Sister Faustina was sent to visit hell to be able to explain what is happening when you go into hell. Souls are on fire, but they never finish to burn. It is of terrible pain and torment.

I went through the open golden doors. Golden miles-long gates. I went several times and for consecutive nights. I visited heaven, where the colors are much more vibrant, the air is pure, the birds are singing a love melody and even streams of water are music to the ears, streets are paved with gold, and we have to continue to fight until everyone makes it. Because right now ...

Parhedron the Typhon is here, in this "Ibehave mental hospital" place. I was the only one to see him here, but they all saw me choking. I had to fight him. I have to go; I have to go. "I love you." And he hung up.

Three days later I received another call from him very early.

"VIE that time they took all my clothes off and left me for three days naked in the room. I knew that you were worried, I heard your phone calls and them telling you that I was sleeping. I knew that you would know better but I could not get to the phone naked, I love you, and talk to you soon"

One week passed that time before I heard again from him

Hi, VIE, please take notes, for a few days since I talked to you last, I have been in a gown, and then they gave me back my clothes. Today, the nurse suddenly violently stripped me of my clothes, dragged me out of my wheelchair under the shower, dumped me on the tile floor, and beat my skull down on the floor saying; "so how does it feel, do you like it." Then a big guy came and while I was away from my chair still on the floor punched me many times in the face. My face is all swollen and I have the shape of an egg for a forehead. He said that he is a Pastor.

I could hear someone in the background while we were on the phone screaming:

"But I am a reporter, I do not belong here. Let me out immediately! Do you hear me? You better let me out right now."

So, I asked, CHADD what is going on?

CHADD: They admitted a reporter and you heard everything that he said.

The following day.......

CHADD told me "I told him the story of my life, my long history battling the system and the drugs, my black eyes, how I got a Z cut surgery of my tendons for no medical reason while I was in a coma to the reporter, and I made him cry"

Christ is guiding us to see that we must reach beyond the stars to receive and bring forth the Light. We have to break through the third archon, Hekate, and also the fourth, the equivalent of breaking through the fourth dimension of time. We will then begin to inherit eternal life when we learn to break through our linear time dimensions by understanding his power.

Christ told us that the fourth order is the Greek "Typhon" which is the destructive winds and murder of Osiris. Osiris is his alter-ego who can ascend from the earth into the heavens, while Typhon only has the power to hold down the matter. Typhon's primal force is connected with self-willed in opposition to the Truth, the Wisdom, and the Light. The souls that this dark force steals away spend over a hundred and thirty years with him, in hell, until they are destroyed. Typhon is a very powerful dark and satanic force, who commands many, many demons, and these are the ones who entered humanity to attract adultery, fornication, and the ceaseless practice of intercourse.

Chapter 6
Time Traveling Through Sacred Geometry Structures

It seems that we entered the center of the Creation. I feel a deep vibration of love there and a return to a Knowing, a re-awakening to the fact that once one belonged here and that one has traveled here many times in dreams but did not realize it before. Everything is so pure and so rarefied, so perfect and pure, so big and very small at the same time.

Archangel Metatron explained now:

Sacred Geometry structures have the power to initiate dimensional journeying. They amplify the energies of the cosmos into this dimension, opening up portals within space-time that are accessible to those of a high enough vibration. The Sacred Geometry Icosahedron is very helpful in becoming more conscious of one's relationship with the Source, and those who are receptive to the energy will be able to access the vibration of Christ's Consciousness through the power of the Icosahedron. The Icosahedron is the main structure of energetic amplification, and the dodecahedron has the effect of instigating dimensional transport.

The work, for ascending, is to begin by building the 3D Earth Merkabah within Your light body through the opening of the heart chakra and you need the du Messie couple to reconnect you. (All beings vibrating at the level of the heart chakra will automatically achieve this. You have been disconnected from it, and you must be reconnected to it).

The next task is to build the 5th dimensional Earth Merkabah, Metatron's cube, within Your light body. The Metatron's cube is a compound of all five Platonic Solids combined. The Metatron's Cube represents the Feminine, and the straight lines represent the Masculine. Metatron's Cube represents the interlacing together of the Male and female polarities to create the ONENESS field of the infinite ALL there is. The next stage is to be able to access the Central Sun Portal, to prepare for the Ascension of the Body into 5D and Your Return to Immortality. The incorporation of 5-pointed stars into the pentagonal faces amplified the energies of our own Sun. Which is predominantly a 5th dimensional Star and much larger stars have an energetic wake extending across more dimensions. From here on, you are ready to begin accessing Star Gates. Christ consciousness, the Heart, and your Light body.

Chapter 7
Katherine Call For Help

One night I had this vision in a dream.

Carlos knew that CHADD would never agree to marry his ex-girlfriend, but it was the excuse to beat him up under the camera.

The reality is not nicer. The beating served the scenario, Carlos, and Katherine.

Katherine felt that she was losing ground. She, in her reptilian way, was looking for vengeance. How could her stepson find his way and break free?

She did not care about anything else; it was becoming an obsession since she discovered that he was going to find his way to freedom -out of her control. She took her car and left so rapidly that while backing up the car she did not see the little shiatsu and killed him.

She was obsessed with the thought that she had to talk to Paul about it, knowing how jealous he was of CHADD, and after a discussion on the subject, they decided that the best would be to have CHADD get a good beating by the FBI as a teaching lesson and to get information from him.

She contacted Carlos, her son Paul's good friend, and they made a deal, this is how CHADD ended up bruised at the emergency room with a broken sternum. He was a money-maker for everyone and particularly for her. He was a tool and her Puppet to play with in the dark.

But what Carlos was not ready to hear came a few days later.

CHADD went back to pick up his personal belongings left at Carlos's house the night the beating happened and told him " I forgive you" and shook his hand. What a lesson! But did he understand it?

Chapter 8
The Warning: An Attempt to Decapitate the God Duo

The Secret Government did not know that day that CHADD and I switched cars. I was driving his Limited and he was driving my German S car drive I was following him closely when I saw an 18-wheel truck backing up on my four-wheeler's car before making its left turn and driving away.

From where I was, I could see that CHADD was not moving but sitting still. I drove to pass him and stopped at window length and saw that luckily, he had not been hurt and decided to run after the truck that was going away. The driver made me a sign saying that he was going to park. By the time I parked myself, he had disappeared in the back of the runner truck.

I finally approached him. He was wearing an American Veteran hat, and his hands were shaking.

I told him that he backed up into my car and CHADD. But he denied it all. Then he finally came up with a cell phone and took a picture of the front and the back of the car.

Then, a man came out of the building where the accident happened, his phone in hand, and told me:

I saw everything from the office, we have a camera, and it has all been recorded and I have already called the police.

A black female Deputy Sheriff came and took a lot of time talking back and forth to everyone until she finally told us that she had to leave and that she had called the troopers to handle the report. And again, it took a lot of time for the troopers to come. About 4 hours later we were still outside of the car, in the hundred Fahrenheit heat with no air condition, sweating and waiting for the trooper's report.

I became suspicious and asked the Trooper for his card and identity. He refused to give me his card but told me:" Look at my badge. I am Master I-V (i5) This is my name". He had sitting next to him a man in a civil outfit with dark glasses and was looking straight ahead all the time.

Who was this silent man? What was he doing in the trooper's car?

Was he even real? Or one of them observing the scene?

Chapter 9
Mind Alteration

Next time you see a "surveillance" camera you will understand the real purpose. It is not to protect you or the public like they want you to think, but it is for their production.

There is a small percentage of evil people who can work with satanic forces and are to control free will and independence. They want world control.

They want to see how they are going to watch their experiment in building a new illusion.

These dark forces that go by code names, like Master I-V (i5) with a film production to see how their energies are working with mind alteration.

These dark energies can see your past, present, and future and they cannot create but can alter your creation and they can alter your journey!

They are working through all elected officials, from Church leaders, Media, Courts, hospital managers, doctors, security, guards, Ministers... and laughing at us.

But in fact, the Government is afraid of Spiritual Knowledge, consciousness, and awareness. They only know that they cannot control this power. They are aware of the power of the reunion of the God Duo and aware of their power but do not know what to expect from them.

So, they created chaos and a mess in CHADD & my lives, they tried to scatter our work, they tried to drain my energy, and tried to bankrupt me. Trying to scatter the power to change their plan with the new world order of reducing the population and keeping human beings in slavery.

And they programmed my blue flame to manipulate him and make him act and look insane in their film production.

The black government court ordered him to an assisting facility, extorted all his money under the table in cash, and then made him be reevaluated many times in mental hospitals while the insurance company kept paying the hospitals.

Can they win the battle by manipulating him and creating chaos in my life?

Here is the answer: Warning to the secret Government from the Galactic Federation Fleets.

Chapter 10
A Galactic Federation Fleets Message... A Warning to the Secret Government

To begin with, our fleets are positioned in three rings. The first ring surrounds Mother Earth and her artificial companion, your Moon. This fleet contains over one million ships, most of which are small, unarmed scout and transport vehicles. Their task is to observe you and your world, to oversee fleet operations, and to transport certain types of supplies that cannot be teleported to our bases. Our bases, located beneath all of your continents, oceans, and seas, are linked to a vast array of crystal cities and communities that comprise Inner Earth. Yet another group of bases is to be found on your Moon, which contains a huge network of command and research facilities. These stations provide the means for us to monitor your secret government's collection of space, time, and inter-dimensional weaponry. They pose no potential threat to us.

Surrounding this first, or inner ring are several spokes that consist of several special liaison and defense fleets. Their purpose is, first, to supervise and then, to take effective countermeasures whenever necessary. Our purpose is to refuse your secret government's continued use of any weaponry that may pose a threat to our earthly allies. We have set up interplanetary 'stations' to close any inter-dimensional star gates and to carefully monitor any artificially created distortions in time's natural waves.

They set up interplanetary 'stations' to close any inter-dimensional star gates and to carefully monitor any artificially created distortions in time's natural waves. Here, bear in mind that physicality is an illusion created by its inhabitants' collective core belief and the dictates of the divine plan. In this, natural patterns occur in the way Time and Light coalesce to form 'space' — the stuff that produces realities. Dark, limited-conscious societies have used these natural patterns to construct fearsome weapons that alter realities, mutate dimensions, and warp or constrict the flow of time.

Your secret government has co-opted the work of many of your inventors and scientists and merged it with several off-world technologies.

Other secret government technologies are capable of altering your physical, mental, and emotional bodies. Their vile purpose is to bring about the eventual control of your minds. Then, they can complete the genetic alterations left undone by the fall of Atlantis some 13 millennia ago. Our mission is to neutralize and prevent any large-scale adoptions of these technologies. Every day, Heaven is working to finish, on schedule, the long process that will return you to full consciousness.

Once again, we put on warning those in your secret government who continue to harbor the belief that they can hinder this sacred operation. We WILL NOT tolerate such attempts. Accordingly, we have established a full team of scientists and corresponding liaisons who are on the lookout for these programs and are then limiting their effectiveness. Properly applied, these technologies can substantially assist what Heaven is creating. Dear Friends, we most sincerely welcome a full disclosure of the covert acts, committed during most of Earth's last two centuries, that have hindered your return to full consciousness. We are here to break through the veil of forgetfulness, forgetfulness that every single soul dwelling in a human vehicle here on earth is a CREATOR of their own lives, is in control of their reality, and CAN change anything and everything to experience what they wish to experience. We are here to activate the grids, activate the portals, and activate humanity and GAIA as a whole. We are here to illuminate, transmute, transform, assist, and make way for a new peaceful, harmonious understanding of life. We are here to open the doorway for humanity to enter into a coalition with our star families to CONSCIOUSLY be part of the process of creation. To consciously understand that what happens on Earth affects everything in the cosmos. We are here to bring peace, through the understanding of SELF. We are here to be the way showers to show by example what any soul dwelling on earth is capable of!"

Chapter 11
Fifteen Days Later

CHADD goes into a hypnotic trance, at regular periods, for many days in a row and someone is manipulating his brain, and he always ends up in a rehabilitation center. Either 6 or 8 policemen came, they beat him, handcuffed him, pushed him into the car and he was driven to Ibehave. Some other times one ambulance came, they tripped him on the bed, put a ball in his mouth, and drove him to Ibehave.

Through drugs and alteration of his brain, they manipulate him. One time, visibly acting like a robot he was breaking glasses on the floor unable to hear me.

Another time he was forced to travel back to another realm to meet a model and wanted to leave the country with her, but she was invisible, and then Fallen Angels attacked him. I could see the bites on his skin. On that particular episode of hypnotic trance, a Pastor introduced him to a girl, and a few nights later I received clarification of what it was.

The archon "Pastor Darkin" was guiding him to this girl who was a created illusion.

I worried I needed to understand. What was this for?

I entered into a deep meditation that guided me to receive this vision. I found myself in front of the Pastor. It was the end of the office, and some people were making the line in front of me to check hands with him. I decided to do the same. When my turn finally arrived to shake hands with him, he acted as if I was invisible even though I said Good morning. His eyes were looking fixed at me, much more focused on trying to possess me and I was not welcome here. The vision switched rapidly, and I was still in the archon Church caught between two front entrance sliding doors. The only one that was unlocked and opened was the one going outside, but to get back to my car I had no choice but to go back through the inside Church to access the parking lot. The unlocked door was opening to a big pipe that was rejecting some muddy green water of horrible smell coming out from the church in a retaining pond.

At Christmas time CHADD gave all of his furniture to the Church. His black crocodile leather sofa and all his computers and TVs. As handicapped in a wheelchair, he called someone to come and pick it up from his car. Once the car was unloaded, he saw the Church Security coming towards him. He began, as usual, to smile, and said hello to him, but in return for a hello he was asked to leave the premises NOW! and was escorted out of the Church property. He left in shock. Not even six months ago he was invited by him to a Freemason lunch in his church.

Later on, that week he received a phone call from Pastor Darkin from the church asking to meet him at the wine and cigars place, while he was with Carlos's neighbor. But CHADD had his intuition telling him to be careful and he went on purpose to the wrong location. Pastor Darkin called him back wondering where he was. He finally joined them and what followed later on at night left him in reflection and wonder.

He went that night to visit Carlos, this was before the beating, and he saw on the back of the track of Carlos' neighbor, a neurologist Andrew Nuvel whom he met this morning with Pastor Darkin, his gifts to the Pastor's church.

It was confirming what I saw previously. Dark forces are using this particular church and its church leader and this particular Pastor Darkin to mislead CHADD and us. His goal is to make him mix his blood with some fallen Angels. So that fornication could occur.

Chapter 12
The Key to a Yellow Lamborghini Car

While the car was in the repair shop after the attempted murders our insurance company made a reservation for a rental car at the Happy-land Resort location to a rental car company, and CHADD drove me to the VIECH to pick up the car.

No one was there to serve me.

After 5 minutes of wait, CHADD decided to check the front entrance of the Hotel.
He saw his cousin passing by and shouted out her name, Lora! Lora!

She could not possibly have heard him, but she ignored him and continued on her way.
CHADD was not at the end of his surprises that day.
A woman approached him with a little 5-year-old boy who handed him the key to a beautiful green Lamborghini and told him to sit inside the car with her son on his lap as she wanted to take their picture together.

This is when I came to find him. The hotel Valet who was also the Security man handed me the key with a name on it and told me "Here is the key to your car take it and you know now where to go. Go!"

I rapidly understood that someone was trying to get us in trouble. But for what reason was I thinking? I replied to the man "No, this is not my car, but the man insisted, and I said Stop do not insist" as he continued insisting.

Then I told CHADD to come with me as the rental car employee was probably back at her desk and that my car could be ready. And he followed me.

But trouble continued. I came to the entrance of the rental car company to find, stopping me from approaching the front desk 3 men arms crossed on their chests. Two impressive by their sizes Sheriffs and the Hotel security men that handed me the Key. I decided to address right away what could be the problem by saying to the middleman security " By the way, did you find who was trying to get me in trouble and handed me a car key that was not mine" to which he replied, " Nobody handed you any Keys to a Lamborghini car."

I then bypassed them and went to see if I could get my rental car. The girl began to make it very difficult for at least one hour. First, she said that there were no rental cars to find booked under my name. I had to look into my files to find my adjuster's name and phone number and called her. But I had her voice mail.

I left a message and 30 minutes later she called me back, explaining that it could not be. I was at the right location and my reservation was made and confirmed. Then followed a back and forth, passing phone hands to hands between the rental car employee, me, and the insurance company adjuster.

You would think that this was all, but no.

The employee began to give me a hard time. Telling me that she could not take my ATM card but only a credit card which I did not have with me. I began to argue as it made no sense to me. I was hungry and tired by the heat. I arrived at 9 AM and it was 3:30 PM.

Finally, I got a taxi and went home, took my credit card and, back to the rental car to take possession of my rental car.

Twenty minutes after I was back home, I received a strange anonymous phone call.

"Your co-worker is driving his car like a maniac, you should tell him to slow down" I heard a click, and he hung up" I was wondering what that was now.

Thirty minutes later I received another phone call "The car has been totaled; I have seen everything from the animal clinic window. I have seen the crash, but the driver is not hurt. It is at the corner of Lake Magnolia and Pines Ave" Then click again.

I rushed to the garage into the rental car, drove to the place indicated, and found CHADD already out of the car, he grabbed the door of my rental car and rushed into it.

CHADD still in trauma from the incident began to tell me what happened:

"The car accelerated by itself and became out of control up to 135 MPH. I tried everything to slow it down, but nothing worked, and I had to crash it into a ditch to stop it. And, the weirdest thing that happened, is that a man "strangely" looking like Willy the famous actor passed by the VIECH and told me: "Hey man I could not have done better, and we have it all on camera as I was following you very close"

Later on, my guides told me that it was a well-known actor with three Academy Award nominations, and CHADD had been used as a stunt.

Willy was being paid a fortune while CHADD forced to risk his life was not.

I rapidly finished parking the car on the side and went to see the VIECH. The first thing I saw and that bothers me the most was that no airbags had deployed during the impact and the front right tire was destroyed.

Suddenly a man with a strong Spanish accent appeared from nowhere and spoke:

"Let me help you move the VIECH onto the side as it is in the way of traffic."

He tried to start the car, but the engine refused to run, so he asked me to sit in the driver's seat and to make sure that I would turn the wheels to the right side while he would push the car.

And he disappeared the way he came before I could ask his name or thank him.

This brought a reflection to CHADD a few days later and he said:

The Government is using us to make a movie.

"Willy, the Golden Globe-winning actor told me: I was so close I got it all on camera I could not have done better man?"

Indeed, the Reptilians and archons, the secret Government, are controlling human beings and using them as their slaves but also as experiments through cameras placed everywhere. Through the TV screen and the cameras posted in every building and public place, where they watch and observe our acts and reactions to what they implant in our minds and make money on us.

First, they keep you in a sleeping state with chemtrails, drugs, mental facilities, etc...Then when they can they chip you with vaccines or lasers in various places then they manipulate you like puppets to finally analyze their strategy, to be able to exploit human beings even more.

And what is better than using CHADD and VIE, if they can for very specific tasks? Why not use CHADD as a stuntman in dangerous action for free? Through medications imposed by the court on CHADD and his various stays in Hospitals, nobody will trust him.

This is what they have imprinted in his brainwashed mind in the last 5 years, with the cooperation of his acquaintances and archonic family and of course Paul.

But this is not my case, and I can see their manipulation and the effects on my blue flame and I...

Chapter 13
ASHTAR COMMAND
"The Airborne Division of the Great White Brotherhood"

That reminded me of the story of a woman named Amelie who took an appointment pretexting that her husband did not want a child and she had to have a traumatic abortion now she could not get pregnant, and she was searching for a solution and needed to see me.

I remember having intuitively protected the entire office with the Violet flame of Saint Germain and when she arrived her husband came to the door with her. I saw the dark of his eyes rolling and he was not able to look at me directly, but also, he never could pass the entrance and penetrate inside the institute.

When Amelie passed the door and entered my office, I could not believe what I saw.

I began to wonder from which epoch she could be coming from.

She was wearing a ridiculous outdated and never-before black hat and some lacquered black vinyl-looking shoes with a bow tie on top. The top of her white outfit was all embroidered and the black skirt was without form.

At her second appointment, she mimicked receiving the holy communions and pretended to see many Angels. And it went on for a few sessions. She would get on her knees and pretend to receive holy communions each time and I was waiting to see where all this comedy would lead us.

Until one day, thinking that she could take me by surprise, I felt that dark heavy energy coming.

But the surprise was hers.

I rapidly protected myself and retracted my energy but also rapidly telepathically called Ashtar Command (Commandant Ashtar Sheran) to act and take care of the situation.

And here is what she commented out loud:

"Oh! Oh! What is happening? It is so scary. Who is this big scary man? His eyes are … Oh! His hands are powerful like a weapon. I saw a tall and impressive man, looking like a centurion, one of his guards processed him, he violently pushed the door wide open for him and respectfully moved himself out of the way to let the impressive man inside the office"

Two weeks after this session she called me and said: I have many Angels in my apartment, and some have their wings broken. It is like leaking green from the wounds and they look down from my balcony very sadly. I have so many of them that it is too crowded. I would like to bring them to your office. To which I replied certainly not. I never saw her again after that. She e-mailed me saying that my therapy was not for her.

He entered the emergency room on a Sunday 7/27 at 1:30 am and was transferred to the Ibehave on Friday 8/1st.

For fourteen days his physical body was here but he was time traveling in other dimensions. He could not eat or take a shower. He could not transfer himself from his bed to the chair and I could finally communicate with him again by the fifteenth day.

While he was out of his physical body, and in another realm, he saw the secret Government at work.

On the second following Friday, he (CHADD) asked me to come and meet Dr. Ming at the Ibehave facility. Doc Ming wanted to ask me questions. I went but instead of an interview with the Doctor, I was introduced to a small office to visit him. His coordinator, a young woman originally from Taiwan entered the office room to ask me a few questions regarding his case.

And that was "THE" great opportunity for me to tell the truth. And I told them "I know everything that is happening inside this hospital, and it is a breach of the Fifth Amendment of the Constitution."

So, I was aware of everything before it happened. The weekend passed and I received a phone call from CHADD saying:

"VIE, you have exposed the entire situation concerning the Judge. He is not a judge anymore and he does not know how to react. The whole truth is known. The system has trapped itself once again thanks to you"

Then he left his body again, went first to take a look at the moon, then visited the interplanetary stations. Saw the work of the dark limited conscious societies, the secret Government technologies able to alter the physical, mental, and emotional. The warning of Ashtar Sheran Command.

Then he came back in his body with all the necessary information, and he witnessed that the

Ibehave rehabilitation center was doing the same to patients admitted.

Sunday the 3rd he could place a phone call, but this was short as again they cut us off.

On Monday the 4th, he was cut short by 2 phone calls that he made when he tried to communicate with me. Today, Monday Carolina contacted me, expecting that I would have access to his bank account and could handle her in cash from his account his monthly SS disabilities check that she had to give to the court authority. To Mr. Slown and Judge Forest. So, I took the opportunity to tell Caroline that they would not allow me to have any phone conversation with him.
14 days later, His physical body was here but he was time traveling in other dimensions, I could not communicate with him again on this dimension but only on the other one.

He time-traveled to dimensions where he could oversee the secret Government intentions. Saw the work of the dark limited conscious societies, the secret Government technologies able to alter the physical, mental, and emotional.

Then he came back in his body to admit that it is what is done to human beings that are admitted to Ibehave rehabilitation center and that we needed to have more people aware of it before admitting their own families and that we finally work to close all these facilities.

A Very Important Message from Marie Madeleine to Humanity

Implanted cameras, Governmental movies, and mind control on gifted souls, these people who cannot just be who they are. The illusionary implanted world and the distortion of your reality.

They created fear through war and the torture of Christians. They feed themselves on your emotions. Religion, science, and the medical industries have been labeling and identifying who does not fit into the typical roles of societies. Instead of a human being who deserves equal rights, happiness, and life they are labeled with "mental illness" They have been tagged by the secret government, the dark energies, which are interfering with their lives.

Under the rules of this secret government, they are abused, oppressed, and deprived of free will and freedom. Some of them have no more identity, no credit history, and no money and are unable to survive by themselves with no car, no phones, and no home. They have become the subject of the Government, county, and state. And it is all about mind control on gifted souls.

Millions of people recognize that humanity has been misled and deceived regarding the presence of a large population of human beings on this planet, and the deception is from the Devil. Those who preach that money is the source of all evil are part of the one that controls the planet, and they are the ones who worship money. This is a good pretext to control human beings through the reduction of the human population and reducing the others as slaves.

Most of you, when do you have time to take vacations and enjoy life? Don't you have to work more and more to pay your bills? Have you visited one of these mental places? The Fifth Amendment of the US Constitution is in breach.

It is time to awaken and to stand for yourself, for the planet, and your brothers and sisters. Do not be an observer anymore, act or stay in slavery. Only seven Angels are left on the planet. Get busy now!

Chapter 15
Greetings from Another Realm

From another realm: "Greetings all of you,

As we, human beings, embark on our journey we choose our parents and our play for our growth and to do our part of the planetary play. We, meaning you, came to learn and to graduate to the next level.

Human beings never come with their complete body. We leave a few, of us in different parallel dimensions.

This is what Scientists did not quite understand yet. And this is part of the confusion with mental illness diagnostics. We are holographic bodies of Light and to stay manifested we are in a geometric form called a tetrahedron.

Physically we live in an illusionary world. It is the planetary play where each one has a piece of the puzzle and its part to play.

This planet Earth belonged to the Pleiadians. Today the human population is a melting pot of a mix of various planets' beings. At one point the Pleiadians lost the intergalactic battle, and the population comes from a human lab experience.

Pleiadians are partners with the Sirians. Sirians are the guides for the consciousness of the sun in the Galactic night. Pleiadians and Sirians both work with the temples in Egypt. The Sirians hold the records and secret knowledge while the Pleiadians work to open the hearts.

After that, an unidentified flying object, crashed on a ranch northwest of Roswell, New Mexico, sometime during the first week of July 1947 an exchange contract was signed by the Government with aliens. It was agreed on some exchange between a quota of human beings for experimental purposes in exchange for more advanced technologies.

Today the secret Government in power, the black Government (also called Illuminati) which likes to call itself the third world order has the objective to reduce the human population to control and enslave it better. This is achieved with the use of the advanced technologies they acquired.

With the ascension process, the Merkabah must be activated.

At the time of ascension, only those that have more strands of DNA reconnected will make it. The body will not support going from a few strands to two thousands of DNA at once.

The secret Government through their chosen leaders in Churches, media, hospitals, Courts, etc... maintains the population unaware of the gravity of their activity and the consequences. They lie and withhold information or release false information.

Chemicals have never cured anything, and they are poison to the body. They created and owned the pharmaceutical companies on purpose.

Illnesses and diseases are created. Mental illness is created. Most people mentally ill and diagnosed insane are people that have access to other realities, they are more aware, and they act of course differently to the standard.

They have already more strands of DNA reconnected, and they can access some knowledge that others cannot. Therefore, they do not fit society, their agenda. They remember who they are and what they are for, what mission they are here to accomplish, and the majority of society judged, labeled them, and maintained them in drugs in mental facilities, because of their "behavior" and their different way of understanding things.

Some humans have been chipped and these chips are linked to a satellite from where these people are under mind control and manipulation. These are the ones that are used to accomplish horrible suicides, crimes, and shootings, acting in a foggy state and a trance.

There are only two categories: One the secret Government (lost Souls and dark energies) they cannot win and the second category the winners.
Our Government has more powerful and advanced technologies.

CHADD & VIE's mission is to guide as many Souls as possible during the ascension time. They are two five-star Generals and failing is not an option.

CHADD & VIE are empowered and came to help you. They have the ankh and the keys of Enoch and work for us, the Highest Government of the Universe. They have the wisdom and the knowledge. The secret Government, their helpers, and their allies are trying hard to stop them and their planetary mission. They are using their helpers and allies to deprive them of resources and freedom.

But CHADD & VIE cannot be defeated.

Chapter 16
Chateau Asylum

I was driving my car along the ocean beach; it was a beautiful day. The water was turquoise, with no wind and no waves. I could see through it the white sand, the corals, and the fish. Suddenly entered a vision. I am looking at...

That time I, went to research what was going on with the pharmaceutical companies and the drug companies. I wanted to investigate a little bit more about these growing numbers of places called rehabilitation centers, and behavioral and mental hospitals.

I visited a few of them in my dreams.

The "Chateau Asylum" gained a pretty bad reputation long ago, but it is in reality not so different than most mental institutions around the country. But those institutions didn't have an amazing history like Chateau. Chateau Asylum has a remarkable past. Its story reveals more–political scandals, patient abuse, use of treatments such as ECT and lobotomies, and the incarceration of thousands of men, women, and children who weren't mentally ill at all. I was able to see those who have been convicted of a crime but who are considered mentally incompetent to stand trial.

And what I found out is so unethical and unacceptable. It is all about torturing before destroying Earth and its inhabitants.

These lost souls are working hard to eliminate and exterminate the Earth's population through drugs, lack of freedom, and control. They all make money in the process. Military, kids, hospitals, doctors, pharmaceutical companies, rehabilitation places, courts, lawyers, etc...

Waters are polluted with pharmaceutical drugs disregarded in trash, and restrooms.

I entered the office of the Doctor and manager in charge. I was curious to see what was in it and how he was working. I found a book open on a list of questions and that was enough to confirm what I thought and knew. There is no psychiatric test that can prove mental illness, but the DSM IV (i5?) is no more no less than a simple checklist of questions from which depends on the name of your illness and the drugs that you will be prescribed.

It is not as if there is some study of tissue of the body or matter. It is an all-made-up category.
All these fancy psychiatrist names are simply made up. These disorders do not exist in matter.

It is simple marketing. It has nothing to do with science. In meetings psychiatrists and pharmaceutical Companies decide what disorders to list in the next DSM. All disorders given names have financial ties to pharmaceutical companies. Mental illness is a scam.

Chapter 17
God Asked Me to Read the Future in the Light

God commanded me to drink the blood of Jesus and to listen to a very specific frequency of Sound music on my modified speakers by CHADD.

It did not take me long at all. All was so vivid and harmonious. So much Love and Joy. I was in complete harmony possessed by the Holy Ghost and so well guided.

I first saw colors that no one sees with human eyes. Then the company of my spiritual family, my helpers, guides, and protectors arrived. The father, of course, was there, Mother Mary, Jesus, Saint Hildegard of Bingen, Sister Faustina, Mother Theresa, Monk Thomas Morton, my ancestor Pierre Montour de la Roue, Archbishop Fulton Sheen, the Tibetan Monks were the first to join us, followed by the Australians' aborigines, the Indians' Eagles, the Mayans were there too, and all the celestial helpers were there to assist.

And I predicted the future by reading the light. It was an intense and magnificent moment. I was in a great trance with the Holy Spirit, and I began to predict the future.

I predicted the change and the freedom of the planet. I kept saying "We are free. Freedom is here. We made it, we are victorious in Christ. Love conquered all. The Earth is free"

I could observe the truth of every person on Earth. I saw all sisters and brothers in the human Family and the most recalcitrant souls. Also, all precious children of God, no matter how far their behavior patterns, or their life experiences may have been from reflecting the truth. I felt all of the painful human miscreations associated with these Children of God as innocent primordial energy.

Then, in perfect Divine Order, they were set FREE to live and to co-create the patterns of Love, Oneness in reverence for Life associated with the New Earth.

Chapter 18
Key to Inherit the Light Kingdom

Understand that we have set up a plan to clear the dark from all aspects of Creation, not only this Cosmos but way beyond it. This plan was set up long ago. Whilst the focus of most of us has been bringing forth a change in consciousness on this planet, the shift triggers an advancement for all Creation that will represent the end of the dark's reign anywhere.

The set-up game is that we would be present in this consciousness; the dark would know that CHADD was to trigger this shift and they believed that they would be able to destroy him and his mission and that nothing in this consciousness could stop them. Except that I have received the KEY that they didn't imagine could exist in this dense consciousness, and when they came forth, I was able to clear them.

This process has been going on, now, for nearly nine years, a process we thought would be over by now. But it has continued, though we have made progress.

The dark entities have to be dealt with because this clearing has been less about this planet than Creation in general. It is to clear all expressions of the dark from everywhere in Creation.

The attacks by these dark entities have been about the transition in consciousness on this planet and beyond.

The nature and scope of the interference has changed massively over time. What we deal with today is very simple in comparison to the situation we had to face in the past. No one knows how difficult this has been for my blue flame and me.

Luckily, I can use the magic KEY now without defeating the purpose of this time of preparation, which is to clear all expressions of the dark from everywhere in Creation.

Chapter 19
The Ambush

We had passed the check-out time, and I went to extend his stay. They knew us by now and knew that we wanted to extend the stay for a few more days. But when I came to the front desk, I heard sorry it is fully booked and you have to leave as soon as possible.

I did not quite understand but went up and packed everything.

Antoinette (the Haitian cleaning woman) did not understand either.

'You are not posted on my board for checking out today but 2 days later!"

CHADD was in prayers and battling the demons on another level with no sleep for four days, His eyes were red, and it was hot. I did not know what the next step would be. I went around town with him sitting next to me figuring out what was planned for the day, and he was silent in a trance. From time to time, I could hear mumbling.

By noon I received a phone call from Carolina.

She said by the end of the day I will need to meet you both at the usual place. Time passed by, and she kept telling me that she was sorry but that it was an important review case and that she would come as soon as it was finished.

Finally, 8 hours later she called to say that she was on her way.

Suddenly, from the parking lot where we were parked, I saw a man running in the direction of his car with an eight-year-old little girl under his arms. The little girl was screaming" Help me! He is not my father! He is not my father! Mommmmyyyyy! Please help me" He dropped her and fell on the grass with her rapidly putting his hand on her mouth and maintained her on the soil with his other hand. Several Men from the Italian restaurants rushed out and crossed the road in the direction of the kidnapping and one man released the little and others maintained the man on the soil firmly.

I thought that it was quite weird, how these men from inside the restaurants on the other side of the road could hear her screaming and, a woman the mother, was waving her hands towards the men in a gesture to say, "It's ok, all is well, everything is fine."

It was at that same time of reflection that Caroline called and asked me to follow her. She drove us straight to the Ibehave Center.

I immediately told her about the attempted kidnapping, and she replied: It had to be a mentally ill man from this Ibehave hospital.

CHADD was still in fire with the Lord and still fighting the dark.

He became very agitated, and his face changed. His whole body was trembling. I could read the horror of the battle he was going through on his face when Caroline approached his door and asked him to leave the car and follow her.

Caroline turned herself towards me and said: I have never seen him like that. He is scaring me. I do not understand.

Then she ordered me to move far away from my car while she would admit him to the Ibehave Hospital.

From where I was located, though a good distance from the car I was still able to see what was happening. I recognized the "kidnapper" and saw also the Sheriff from the scene, leaving the "kidnapping" place and moving towards CHADD.

Outside the scene location, on the front of the building and side of the road, was posted a homeless man in a wheelchair with a hat in which was written "Air Force" Who was that man, Why was he here just at that time? I decided to talk to him.

Hi! Did you hear the little girl screaming?

Him: No! Really! What happened? He replied.

This was all I needed to hear. He could not have heard the screams. This was a setup. They needed eight hours to put it together.

And of course! The Regional & Association Psychiatric Center that also owns the "Ibehave Hospital" had discharged CHADD and did not want to admit so easily their defeat the previous Thursday. Indeed after 35 years of battle, from 5 years old, he finally broke from their grip and gained "freedom"

For 35 years they experimented with all the different drugs on the market, used him as a guinea pig, and were forced to admit that he stopped all drugs against their doctor's warning. They warned him all these years that he would die if he decided to stop taking his prescribed drugs after so long but was forced to admit that nothing happened. Now he was what they never expected him to be and a danger to them if he would talk and be believed.

The Psychiatric Center was losing face. They were scared of course. He was the living proof of the psychiatric drugs scam and could sue for malpractice. He was now officially in the right to ask for compensation to the court. Dr. Ganakjam began to be worried. He would lose face and a lot of business. My blue flame life has been taken away, his future, his money. He had not been able to get his own family all these years, he had no credit history built, he had no money, no car, no phone, and no home. All his friends considered him insane. His image was tainted, and his life was ruined. He tried all these years to reach help, even though what he thought was his friend, Pastor Darkin but no one had any time to listen and help him.

He discovered that the Leader of the Church, Pastor Darkin, whom he considered his friend during all these years, had acted many times behind his back to baker him and have him admitted to a mental facility. The Pastor was also friends with a neurologist that poisoned him. And he saw them shaking hands in a parking lot the same morning. He had no idea at that time that they knew each other.

He had some doubts, the water tasted different, and he poured it on the carpet in a semi-circle. It did not take long before the results appeared in front of our eyes. The carpet was bleached in a semi-circle. He rapidly used his senses; he needed to know what was in the tainted water. As soon as he began to have the symptoms, from the ingested chloride, hydroperoxide, and strychnine that was put in his bottle of water, he asked me to drive him to the walking center that was very close to where he was.

We walked in and I was very happy to see that there was no one in the waiting room before us.

The "Pakistani" Doctor Usha Kashin rapidly showed up. I explained to her his situation rapidly and she refused to help us:

"I cannot do anything, he is not my patient, he is all white and there is a lot of damage"

How could she refuse to help? But also, how could she know about any damage? She did not even take care to examine him.

It is Tuesday night, rain is pouring, it is striking like hell, and it is around nine o'clock, I am in Prayer preparing myself for the long meditative prayer night. It is the 5th night the Holy Spirit kept me awake and in prayer. The phone rang and took me by surprise, and now the dog was barking.

I am your Creator. I am Christopher Redemptor. Listen to me Marie-Madeleine, you are my wife. I love you so much. You are carrying my seeds in you. I bought you your island. I am relocating you soon. Tomorrow morning, I want you to take the passports and go to the private airport fifteen minutes from where you are, but first go to the French croissant coffee shop, you will be given... one million dollars to be deposited in the bank account.

Then please come and visit me. I need my wife. Bring me a razor and some shaving cream. Since they got me in this mental hospital, they did not allow me to take a shower and shave.

I have given everything to Berino on the island, and Francesco a blue Lamborghini.

We are leaving this country, no one respected us, they tried to kill me, some authorities have beat me, others dumped me on my head, they poisoned me, the emergency walking center refused to help me, I have been court ordered nearly two years to an asylum and many times to mental institutions for many years. They stole my money; they tainted my name and destroyed our image. They worshiped the devil for power and money. We are living on our island.

Dr. Affia Assam Kalsam and Bitsy of Regional Psychiatric Center are anti-Christ. They are all going to hell now, and all others and their partners in crime are either going to hell or cursed"

Then the phone hung up. Five minutes later the phone rang again.

"Marie-Madeleine, I Love you, and I need you. Do not let me down. See you soon. You are so spoiled; you have the Key."

Chapter 20
My Divine Healing Mission

When I was born, I knew that I was different and so did my Mother. I was trained in the temple of Isis, where I was trained in the mysteries of the great Goddess, the Cosmic Mother. My entire human life was about misperception. I know this may find it difficult to believe that Biblical figures have alien origins, but this is who I am. I was trained to attune my mind to enable me to enter these other worlds through my evolution. It was at that point of training and service that I discovered my roots and origin, experiencing myself as a human woman and I began to fully appreciate my gifts and their challenges.

I unveiled some of my gifts to others to find myself misunderstood and betrayed by their ignorance. I was misunderstood on what I was offering.

My reunion with my blue flame after determination came of my teachers that I was well prepared for the task.

I was now beginning my mission that had been planned and this involved, of course, my Blue Flame. We are on a mission that involves humanity. Like we already did in Atlantis and Egyptian times.

It started with a dream, then proceeded to visions of many feelings. From happiness to sadness, horrors, and deceptions. And deception is from the devil. The fourth order, Parhedron Typhon, the powerful archon under whose command are many demons that enter humanity to entice them into fornication, to steal away souls that must spend many years tormented by demons in his fire before to be destroyed.

I am alone on top of a beautiful hill. As I look at the valley the colors are indescribably vibrant. They are vibrant and alive. It is breathtaking and breathing smells different. I am breathing all these alive colors, and I realized that I felt more alert, much more alive. It somehow induced me a greater energy and lifted me to a place where I was attending to every detail. I am at the same time looking at the landscape downhill and also looking at my painting. Is it an outstanding panoramic scene I am looking at or am I painting it or is it both at the same time? I do not know. It is a little bit of both. It is so beautiful, and I feel so good. I am alone I do not see anyone else with me, but I am very happy and at peace.

Then the next minute, I am looking onto a highway, but that time from a down perspective looking up, what I see is military trucks, only military everywhere, and no civilians. A highway packed with military trucks going on both sides of the road in different directions. Like going back and forth on the highway. In the back of these military trucks are many soldiers with guns.

My phone is ringing now, and the woman I met during the four-day convention is calling me repeating my name before she can talk:

"VIE, VIE, VIE it is horrible I saw it all, there is a military with guns that want everyone to be vaccinated by antibiotic injection or they will be put in concentration camps and will be vaccinated anyway. It is to kill us all, animals and everything. Military are everywhere and also the trees are dying on the island, they are dying due to many chemicals the closest island to it is sinking. The Earth is suffocating, I am afraid, what is going on? What does that mean? It is so real."

A few weeks later now CHADD had also a vision: "VIE, you were right in your vision, I saw it also and even saw more details to it. I saw dead bodies floating in water all over the town. It is full of only dead bodies. No one survived. It is devastating and horrible. It is going to sink underwater, and no one sees it coming."

I was half awake now and I could hear people talking. I listened intently. I am trying to understand but I can't, and they keep talking. I am wondering what they can be talking about. I tried to listen again, but it was too late now I am hearing music. Tibetan monks are chanting.

I turn myself onto my side and I am driving my car now, the road seems to accelerate by itself, the wheels are sliding, and the car is skating on the road, but I still have my two hands on the wheels, and I am in control. The car continues to slide for one or two minutes its course then slowly stops. What was that all about, I think…Who tried to control my car?

I just boarded the plane. I was on a plane without much space, because two obese people came to sit on both sides of my seat, the plane was packed. I fell asleep and suddenly I was awakened searching for air. I looked around rapidly and with my luck was I thinking, that if I called any stewardess for help, they would tell me that the plane was full. What am I going to do? I suddenly had an idea. I turned towards the obese man seated on the aisle seat and told him: Please let me get out quickly I need to go to the bathroom I am sick. When I came back ten minutes later, I asked him if he could exchange his seat with mine and told him I may be sick again and it would be wiser if I moved to my seat. And I felt relief when he accepted.

I had hand-written notes for my next book about some turn of events, things people did, etc. In these notes were many names, and a long list of events past or to come.

After a while, I heard someone speaking in another row. They were talking about my notes, which I no longer had in my possession. I began to recognize who they were by their voices, and I understood now about these two obese people who were suffocating me. It was all a setup.

Now the man with the beer showed a film, a vision animation of a huge structure that was projected over the Universe out the window. They said they had the technology to go to the deepest parts of the universe. They said it was time to stop "them" using this.

Then my vision continued as these feelings filled me, I saw lies, their control, greed and hunger for money, killings, tortures, fears, murders, and it just went on. Then I awoke sweating.

And I am back in the vision again. I am now observing from where I am how they also control and observe through television, electronics, and mental institutions inducing micro currents to induce epilepsy, Alzheimer's, and all these created diseases...

The vision continues and now guidance... My Spiritual family, my guides, and my protectors begin to contact me now. One by one.

"VIE, I am sister Faustina. You have to spread the word for me. It is all about the "Divine Mercy prayer" The world must pray that prayer. It is time, it will save many through this.

It is the prayer for the end of time. It is time. There is no more time. Everyone should hear about it"

Mother Theresa came second. She will help to recover the VAJRA.

Mother Mary came. She is my guide and my protector.

Then my ancestor is happy to see me: "VIE it is me, I am your ancestor, I am Pierre Montour de la Roue. I am with you; I am going to help and protect you and help you with your mission." Pierre Montour de la Roue crest content was a very powerful chevron in the form of an Australian spin back that he uses more or less the way I use my powerful gift from the Tibetan Monk Sarasinian (Sara means without and sinian means sin). He can win any sort of battle with it. He can entangle difficult situations, like cut cords and attachments"

And I heard a very warm voice: "VIE call me Bishop. I am the Archbishop Fulton Sheen. Where I am now, I see it all and what happened to you. I see what they are doing to you. I will not leave you alone anymore. You have my support and help. From where I am I understand better why I have created when I was in a human form, the precious blood of Jesus chaplet. Blood is the consciousness of Life. It is a very powerful chaplet I was guided to create. It is very powerful when you pray on the beads of the precious blood of Jesus. I will always be around you now to help you. I am covering you with my Bishop violet mantel. Just call me when you need me and when you want to pray with me on this powerful rosary of the precious blood of Jesus"

Now "Monk Thomas Merton" is coming around me to help me. Thomas Merton is a very knowledgeable man of the Church, and he is very powerful working with energies and vibration, sound waves. He appears at a very important time to help me. It was just when CHADD was in the asylum and his immune system was getting down, and it was when they were making tests on the vibration of his brain. They were bombarding him with brainwaves, and radio waves. He was exhausted. He came to tell me that he was going to take care of it.

It is about at the same time that Saint and Sister Hildegard appeared also (she is a major twelfth-century mystic and prophet who through her visions all her life hot the source of high information on healing, through a multidimensional approach to the body, and mind, emotions, and spirit) She is with me and she is telling me that I must work with her but also St. Agnes that is now transformed from a Saint to an Angel and her name is now Agni Spiritu" (Patron of the children of Mary. St. Agnes was a Roman girl who was only thirteen years old when she suffered martyrdom for her Faith. Agnes had made a promise, a promise to GOD never to stain her purity. Her love for the Lord was very great and she hated sin even more than death!

I have been given an understanding of the situation.

This was given to me as I went to different denominations to ask for help

I was feeling like a ping pong ball under "some" hands.

First, I reached the Vatican as the Father instructed us to.

I contacted my friend Babette as she was very close to Father Tassim. He recommended me to Father Gillando. I went to the Diocese and left several letters for Father Raymond Gillando, and I learned that he could not talk to me as he was very busy in Court. Then I received a phone call from Father Tassim, and he was excusing himself as he had no help to give me concerning this matter. I thanked him and told him that I understood and left.

But since I spoke to the deceased Pope John-Paul II and asked him for help. I asked him to give a message to Pope Francis and to let him know what the Father told us. And here is what Pope Jean-Paul said to me:

"Greetings Madame, I understand, I will carry the message to Pope Francis"

Driving straight ahead not knowing where I was guided to, I was turning and returning it all in mind trying to figure out what was my next step. I ended up at the Holy Church. I asked if I could speak to any Priest but unfortunately, all had already left for the day and were not reachable. Looking out the window I saw another denomination Church and decided to take a chance. There Pastor Davis was, and I was told that he was going to receive me.

I was nicely greeted, and I began to tell my story my eyes could not have opened wider when I heard this:

"It is very nice of you to have compassion but look at you, you have gone nowhere with it, where did compassion get you? Compassion is leading nowhere but will unbalance you only. Sometimes even handicapped people in wheelchairs must be on the street and find their way. Why don't you let go and let him go? Let him be in the street. It is going to be ok. You'll see. You will be much better."

I thanked the Pastor for his good advice and left horrified. How could a man of "God" tell me to leave my brother in the street without compassion?

I surrounded myself and my energy with the white light protection and the protection of all my Angels and Guides and I asked to be cut from all dark energies in power on this planet and around me. I asked that through my intention they had no choice but to return to the light and then recover their power but until then I intended to cut their destructive power.

I asked them to be guided to all good intentions and knowledgeable people who could help me develop and grow my Business and mission rapidly.

Chapter 21
Visit to the Basilica

In between two admissions of CHADD to institutions I decided, one of these days that he was fighting the demons and was in a trance, to visit the shrine and talk to the Priest. I found a Priest in great pain waiting to confess visitors. I began to tell him that it was several days that he was in this condition, and I was asking for his thoughts, guidance, and benediction. The Priest took a certain time of silence and then said, "Did you ever consider putting him in a mental facility!" I was so horrified that we left without a word.

A few days later CHADD told me that he recognized him and said, "Wait a minute!" He was the Chaplain of the jail I was placed in, before being sent by the secret Government to the concentration camp for 489 days. The Chaplain was at that time in a sheriff uniform and dropped me on the floor on purpose and beat his skull on the concrete several times saying" Let's see what's in this brain. Let's see what's inside this skull."

Six months later I saw the Chaplain again and he could barely walk with a cane!

Then we searched for Angelo-Justino everywhere in the Basilica. We knew that we had to make sure that nothing happened to him. Dark forces were looking for him. We, unfortunately, could not find him, but one visitor told us that he left earlier with one of the parishioners. He was invited to its house for lunch or dinner.

We left but promised ourselves to come back the following day to check on his statute.

Chapter 22
And the Priest Called the Police for Protection

I was driving reflecting on what happened at the BASILICA a few weeks ago. Then I decided to go back. I picked up CHADD and told him to let us go to the Basilica, I felt guided to go back.

We entered and I saw that the Priest at that time was of a little darker completion. I left CHADD and entered the office alone.

"Good morning Father Ravi. Father, I need to talk to you, please. I have a story to tell you. I am not here to ask you for money or anything of the sort, but I need Spiritual help."

Father Ravi "Well! Be brief and quick to the point I do not have much time for you. I am here to confess."

Nobody else was here but us! But I thought he made the point that if anybody shows up confession is his priority.

I began to tell him about the circumstances in which CHADD and I met, handicapped and in a horrible situation trapped by the system, on drugs, with no house, etc...and before I could continue, he pointed to CHADD sitting patiently and praying on his wheelchair outside the office and said:

"I do not believe you"

I was cut in the middle of my phrase and could not believe now what I was hearing. I would never have expected such rudeness from a Priest and a man of God.

Then he went to say, "Do you want to confess now?"

I left him without a word.

I pushed CHADD's wheelchair inside the Basilica and suddenly I felt the energy in my chest, that guidance and sweet energy of comfort, and then was possessed by the Holy Spirit and when my mouth opened it was loud and strong.

With CHADD by my side in the middle of the basilica facing the altar, my arms wide open facing the crucifix, and in a very loud voice I began to talk in the language of the Light. It was obvious that I was delivering a message from God, and he was not happy.

The message took about 10 minutes then we headed towards the door.

The Priest was in the middle of our way out with another man at his side and was on a cell phone disturbed, scared, and calling the Police.

We continued our way out passed the door and passed next to him, CHADD was silent while I was pushing its wheelchair, I said very calmly and loudly without looking at him.

"Father Ravi, get on your knees and pray. This was Mary- Magdelene and the Christ. What the police could do to protect you against the devil if it was?"
And we left and went to eat. We laughed a lot at the idea that the Priest called the police for his protection. We decided that it was better than being sad to laugh at it and that it was hilarious.

Chapter 23
An Old Cosmic Couple

Warriors fighting the satanic invasion of this planet at revelation Bible time, the God Duo, is an old cosmic couple not understood.

Like Jesus was tempted in the desert, CHADD is fighting the dark energies, the dark Government -they keep him in hospitals, court ordered, extortion of money, prescription drugs like Dexedrine amphetamine, and dextroamphetamine.

I had no choice but to protect him at any cost, while he was acting in a way that made no sense and the system took advantage to declare him insane trapping him a little more into dangerous drugs. I did what I had to do as his feminine part God Duo and Biblical companion to protect him.

Dexedrine is a drug given to the military in bombing missions.

Most of his acts were meant to erase the dark forces controlling the system, so the light would take effect. It's like recognizing the fact so that no more energy will remain attached to it.

He had himself possessed at times by evil spirits, for the light to fight them better. He had to play both sides. And I have to stay on his side to help him and guide him back to the light. They know it and try very hard and as much as they can to separate us.

Through his acts, he is saving the children of the planet from the control of the dark. Freeing them from drugs that are trapping them into the matrix and the control of the evil spirits of Mempis the demon with long hair and long tail, with which he swipes the Soul of the people on drugs and amphetamine.

Chapter 24
Fiorella Confession

Fiorella grabbed our attention by displaying French bread and cheese at the organic market. Passing in front of her displaying table she introduced herself to me by "I know you from somewhere! Did we meet at ... was it the last convention in Fort Lauderdale? Chadd asked her if she had children and she replied -I have a little four-year-old daughter and she is not well at all. She just got 5 vaccination shots the same day and her skin is very pale, and you can see all the veins through it. I did not want her to be vaccinated but the authorities have been very forceful about inoculating her or not being admitted at school. I have been wondering if there is a nano chip in the syringe. And now she is very sick, and I am very preoccupied.

She looks pale, is very weak, and her veins are more than should be visible through her white skin. She is very sleepy and breathing like an asthmatic person. I went to the emergency room, but they told me that there was nothing they could do. To just go home and wait until it goes away, and she gets better. But they also said something that worries me. They told me to keep a very close eye on her and not to leave her alone.

CHADD began to narrate her long fight and our Victory that day on the regional county associates all these years on drugs.

I saw her again ten days later and she waved me from the far end of the store. I went to see her and asked about her daughter's health progress. She looked very embarrassed and replied: Oh! Thank you for remembering and asking. She is much better now. She has just had the flu!

That was confirming what CHADD said. This woman was planted to try to get information on what I knew about the vaccinations and their side effects.
A few months later she called us hysterical. I need to talk to you please, please, it's an emergency. But I need to see you in private. Nobody can see me with you.

CHADD and I decided to hear what she had to say. We had an idea, the mysterious way she acted when she requested an appointment seemed to confirm what we thought. So, we told her to come to our office at seven-thirty letting her know that by that time the building entrance would be locked and most people out of work and gone home, and she agreed.

She entered the office with obvious anxiety and was very nervous but five minutes later she began to calm down. She gave us a printed sheet of paper and said: "Look read this first, and we will talk about it after. I know that you are probably already aware of... But I'll stop talking and get silence now until you have finished reading."

We took a look at the paper, and I began to read out loud so CHADD would hear it too.

"A well-known author and Doctor Emeritus Psychiatrist says: That's an epidemic of psychiatric. It's a story and a mythology, it's a fable. It's a scam.

71

The list of the psychiatric mental illnesses names went from 3 to 7 to around three hundred.

Nobody has demonstrated or created a test to show that somebody has a chemical imbalance in the brain.

Psychiatry is an industry of death says another MD.

In the absence of objective medical tests to determine who has ADD or ADHD, doctors rely in part on standardized assessments and the impressions and guardians while the administrators leave little impression room for other causes. These drugs given to the children give them hallucinations and bad dreams.

If a child is "different", and active, he is considered good to be put on drugs.

A mother says that parents will receive as much sometimes, over twelve phone calls the same day until the school calls the parents for a conference. The meeting stands then with the Principal, a Social worker, a psychologist, and the teacher. The parents will hear that they either have to put their child on drugs or the school will put the child in a special school, and that happens as early as 5 - 6 years old.

Here is what Michael Moore said when he was interviewed and asked about the list teachers are following to diagnose the children of ADD/ADHD: Easily distracted - looking by the window- daydreaming..."This was me! I would have been so doped up! After a few minutes, my mind would go into creation."

A Neurologist says, "If the child is stepping out of line, or acting he is put on drugs."

It is widely recognized that there is a strong link between children's bonds to ADD and shared by many when a child is exposed to PCBs and lead.

Normally, children cannot keep attention for more than 20 minutes because when they look at television the brain becomes lazy from the visualization input that they are getting from TV.

Some teachers can tell when children walk at the door that they have been watching Television by their behavior is different. They are acting differently. Parents today are busy with computers and cellular phones and the children are a product of what they see at home.

The pharmaceutical companies have found that there is a big profit to be made playing on the parent's fear and parents' convenience in raising their children.

Another psychiatrist says that six to seven million children are on drugs before they go to school.
These drugs affect the psyche and mind, and they change the brains of children forever and for the worse.

A teacher: As a classroom teacher, we are given nine categories. If a child manifests 6 out of 9, like not sitting steady on his chair – not on task – jumping out of his chair... he must be put on drugs.

General happiness has become medicated and turned into behavior.

What if it is only a list of behaviors?

The main symptoms are nothing else than a list of questions in a manual ICD-10 and DMS IV

A Pastor said that his son has been put on drugs. His son was constantly in a foggy state when he was not sleeping all day unable to live a normal life. With His wife, they decided to try alternative medicine and he said that his son is doing very well now."

Fiorella: I think that when we met at the organic market, I did not fool you, you understood right away. Please do not be mad at me I need to make a living I am a single mother, and this is how I became a social worker and began to work for the Government. They have asked me to get as much information as possible from you. But now all is changed. What you have read is what I found out. I have a little girl at school and the system is applying to my daughter. She is so fragile. She is very weak. Lately, she had so much asthma with allergies I do not think her body is strong enough to survive these terrible drugs. I need your help. I do not know how to handle the situation. Please help me, help my little girl. We need to expose to the public; we need to stop what they are doing to our children, but I cannot do it without you.

Chapter 25
Two Shots of Drugs to Kill

We had a very interesting metaphysical day of work, though very stressful. I did not expect that.

I was not expecting that he would be again used for their movie chasing "Jesus caught somewhere in time" and battling to defeat the devil at the same time.

We entered "la Casa de la Rosa Restaurant" and many "FBI" in Sheriff Uniforms surrounded us. We left and began our chase around town at over a hundred miles, which was very intense due to the local population and cars on the road.

Suddenly out of nowhere two archons in police uniforms stopped us and pointed a gun at both of our faces, on each side of the car. I immediately shouted out "Do not shoot, don't shoot, we are Ministers" to the Pakistani/American policeman on my side.

They immediately jumped on CHADD, grabbed him out of the car, and told me to get out NOW! And sit on the curve of the road on the soil. The rain was pouring on us and in the leather seat of the car. I was wearing white clothes that were now brownish as I was covered by mud, but they did not care. There were lightning and thunderstorms and they pushed CHADD under the shade of a tree. Suddenly I saw a tow company showing up and taking our SUV away while the policemen handcuffed and pushed CHADD in their car, and they disappeared with him. I was still on the side of the road when a third policeman came and told me you could go now "He will call you to update you" and he vanished leaving me in the rain without a car.

Around nine that night, CHADD finally called me to let me know that they institutionalized him, even though they knew that he was a Reverend, and gave him two shots of drugs again, to which he was allergic, and the Doctors were aware. He was not feeling well at all, he was sweating, his heart was beating faster, his tongue was swelling his throat seemed to be almost closed and he was feared for his life.

He fainted and only woke up still sweating to see an insane man on the floor in his room jerking himself then ejaculating on the wood floor.
CHADD was having a hard time breathing and he was feeling very weak. His wheelchair was nowhere near him, and he needed to go to the bathroom. He waited until the morning breakfast time to be able to see someone and request his wheelchair. As no one was near and around previously to observe what the insane man did the nurse went to the conclusion and punished him for food.

Then he was forced to ingest more drugs even though they were all marked as being allergic to in his file. His feet doubled their sizes with the lithium, he had rashes on his arm due to red dye to which he was allergic, and his vision became very blurry. The facility he was admitted was not handicap accessible and he was unable to take a shower. His chair was not passing the bathroom door either.

As if this was not enough, the nurse Natasha forced him also to sign some legal papers, but she knew that he was dyslexic, saying that he had to take the drugs and then sign the papers, or he would not be released.

The 72-hour evaluation hospital turned out to be many consecutive weeks.

He called and asked me to come and meet the Dr. in charge who wanted to talk to me.

When I arrived at the front desk I was asked to sit and wait, which I did. I began to wait patiently as I was intrigued, Why the Dr. wanted to see me? From time to time, I was asking if it would be soon. Finally, after 90 minutes a Chinese woman introduced herself as his nurse in charge Lee Minh, and asked me to follow her in her office. She opened the door to let me in and left me alone for a few more minutes.

When she came back, I asked what was all about and she answered" Oh! The Doctor left already, and I went to find out. He is asking me to interrogate you. He needs some information from you."

I told her me. And she said, "Yes, are you going to take charge of him?"

My intuition told me to be very careful, something was wrong. The Physician requested me to come, I had to wait 90 minutes, and then a Chinese nurse "Lee Minh" going by the name of Sacha is questioning me now.

And she kept asking over and over are you taking charge of him? Suddenly she left and came back with CHADD and told him to keep quiet and shut up. CHADD was very happy to see me, but I could see that he was still fighting the demons. He smelled bad, was not shaved his hair was unclean too. I began to ask questions about his uncleanliness, and I was asked to leave the location immediately.

On my way out followed very closely by Lee Minh, I passed another patient and asked him if he knew CHADD and why he smelled bad and so unclean. He was promptly asked not to answer my question but did anyway and told me: well! This is not a place for his condition with no restroom and no bathroom accessible for him. I was shocked, and left saying congratulations! This is unlawful! I am taking note of it and be very careful, make sure that nothing will happen to him, or you will hear from me.

Chapter 26
The Dark Examination of Mental Illness

I was very relaxed and went quickly into a deep meditation. I left my body, lost track of time, and traveled to the other dimension.

I went to visit my Pleiadian and Spiritual family. I found them at an important meeting reunion.

They were debating on CHADD and similar cases. "CHADD and VIE have been chosen to help people on the planet who are stuck and trapped by the dark secret government in many ways.

CHADD had been chosen to infiltrate all these facilities and the concentration camp as he has spent his life on drugs and survived it. And VIE is outside taking notes of everything that is happening inside.

But what the black court does is that they are trying as much as they can, with their archons' doctors, all these Indians in places, to kill CHADD and they are videotaping everything inside with cameras. They also force him to watch cartoons with subliminal messages and sex programmed by signs and symbols in them.

You know that they are these are dark energies that have re-incarnated now and that infiltrated themselves inside the country taking slowly key places in the medical and pharmaceutical companies. They are the Thuggies. For the members of Thuggee, murder was both a way of life and a religious duty. They believed their killings were a means of worshiping the Hindu goddess Kali, who was honored at each stage of the murder by a vast and complex system of rituals and superstitions. Thugs were guided to their victims by omens observed in nature, and once the deed was done, the graves and bodies were prepared according to strict ceremonies. A sacrificial rite would be conducted after the burial involving the consecration of sugar and of the sacred pickaxe, the tool the brotherhood believed was given to them by Kali to dig the graves of their prey. Thugs were certainly not above robbing their victims, but traditionally a portion of the spoils would be set aside for the goddess. Sir William Henry Sleeman was a sober, no-nonsense Bengal Army officer who from early on dedicated his career to the eradication of Thuggee. Thuggee was unique in transcending all such social barriers. Anyone from a farmer to an aristocrat could be a Thug. Many were even Muslims who, in a truly inspiring feat of rationalization, managed to reconcile their practice of human sacrifice to a goddess with their religion's strict ban on idolatry and murder. They have a tight link with the film production and entertainment industries.

When the police arrested VIE and drove her to jail, the visiting Asian couple took away her VAJRA and brought it back home to Calcutta where they live. We need to help VIE to recover it and help CHADD to free all these patients trapped in drugs that are destroying their neurons. Health insurance is taking a very big role. They keep covering all admissions and it never ends. These mental hospitals, asylums, and behavioral facilities belong to the secret Government, and they are making a lot of money.

Psychiatrists have been involved in human rights abuses in states and all across the globe when the definitions of mental disease were expanded to include political disobedience. Political abuse of psychiatry is the misuse of psychiatric diagnosis, detention, and treatment to obstruct the fundamental human rights of certain groups and individuals in society. It is simply an abuse of psychiatry including one for political purposes.

All these people need neither psychiatric restraint nor psychiatric treatment.

They trap young children, teenagers, etc... in many ways and parents do not understand it.

Like Nicolas who was visiting his aunt from a foreign country and was spending most of his nights looking at TV. When suddenly he began to act weird and scream. He was screaming to his aunt they are looking at me, they want to hurt me ha! They are after me, no stop, stop! Leave me alone and he began to destroy everything inside the house, doors, and chairs, like fighting an invisible person or fighting a ghost.

Nicolas began to be so uncontrollable that his aunt got scared and called 911 to admit him to an evaluation center for mental illness. She did not know what to do and had no clue of what happened to him so suddenly. Dave's story of Janine is another example of what they are capable of. Manipulating people's brains and in fear, when they are separated from the creator and do not acknowledge him.

Governmental and medical institutions code menaces to authority as mental diseases during political disturbances. Nowadays political prisoners all over the world are sometimes confined and abused in mental institutions, and psychiatric confinement of sane people is a particularly pernicious form of repression used by the secret Government in power. Psychiatry possesses a built-in capacity for abuse that is greater than in other areas of medicine. The diagnosis of mental disease allows the state to hold persons against their will and insist upon therapy in their interest and the broader interests of society. In addition, receiving a psychiatric diagnosis can in itself be regarded as oppressive.

Psychiatry can be used to bypass standard legal procedures for establishing guilt or innocence and allow political incarceration without the ordinary odium attached to such political trials. This is a breach of the constitution in the states. It is a violation of the Fifth Amendment.

Now it is expanding to families with domestic problems and disharmony at home and extends to money are common. Parents and families are bakers acting their family members to get "better" by false advertisements and fake promises.

The use of hospitals instead of jails prevents the victims from receiving legal aid before the courts, makes indefinite incarceration possible, and discredits the individuals and their ideas. In that manner, whenever open trials are undesirable, they are avoided.

CHADD is a perfect example; he has been brutalized many times. Once in the middle of his sleep in the facility, he has been deprived of nutrients, and forced to drink tap water with chlorine. They attempted to kill him several times.

VIE Blue Flame has his kidneys borderline to collapse and shut down. He has been given injections and oral drugs that his body is allergic to. It's been too long and too many different drugs, and he already had a stroke from it a while ago.

We need VIE to recover and use her VAJRA immediately and CHADD needs the Ankh around his neck. They all agreed and a month later God decided to intervene.

Chapter 27
Prayers for a Woman in Deep Trouble

Early morning, I was still very preoccupied.

Around 5 am after I passed the night to prayer without sleep guided by the Holy Spirit, I opened my computer and found this

The subject was "Prayers for a young woman in trouble"

Dear brothers and sisters and friends,

Good evening,

Yesterday I met a young person, she is a French European reporter, and we shared our passion for Star Wars.

Her name is Janine.

After we introduced ourselves and began to get into a deeper conversation we came to talk about paranormal phenomena.

She confessed to me all her horrible nightmares, what she was enduring with the brutality and cruelty she was going through every night.

Their bulbs exploded, and pain in their chest like something or someone very heavy was suddenly sitting on the upper part body.

Bruises appear all over her body. Satanic energy is present in her house and everywhere she goes.

She lives alone with a cat, and she is the only member of her family that has not been baptized.

Yesterday I finally was convinced and agreed to make her first move toward God and to say the

"Lord's Prayer" and the "Divine Mercy Prayer" for the first time. She felt already better.

I hope that she will be consistent in her prayer and that all the people who are brutally attacked by satanic energies of that sort.

I am asking for your assistance and your prayers for this young woman.

Thanks to you all,
God bless you.
Dave

A few days later I received another email,

Hello,
Janine has successfully been able to continue to say the Lord's Prayer and she cried a lot the first time. She has slept better lately and has not been attacked since then.

She is not yet accustomed to prayer but since the results and the peace she got from it, she is making her way and getting there, closer, and closer to the Lord slowly.

Thanks to you all again.

God bless you all.
Dave

It is a great example. It is so simple to be saved that people deny it, and the secret is that the Government takes advantage of it. It is time that prayers replace war. Love and compassion for each other take place all over the planet. We will only defeat Satan by honoring and worshiping our creator. Why not? What do you have to lose? Or to gain?

I passed my all week-end on the phone. Another acquaintance was attacked by depression and fear. This is also what the dark energies do. Annette finally accepted the Lord again, but she did not pray and did not believe in it totally and it was enough for the demon to attack her again.

"Faith is the truth

The truth is LOVE and LOVE is the way, LOVE conquers all"

Only LOVE can create. All is created through LOVE. We all have been created through LOVE and the entire Universe has been created out of LOVE by our creator. He loves you; He LOVES all of us, and can't you LOVE him back? Without him, you would not exist and without him, you will lose it.

Get centered now and quiet and take one minute each day in a centering prayer. Call him very gently and see what happens!

VIE

Chapter 28
Padre Pio Comes to Help

After Lenny was sent by the father to deliver me his message that I had finished the battle. He knew that as a long-time warrior, it would be a little bit difficult for me to step out and relax but the time had changed and I had to do nothing now, but to let God take over the situation.

And Padre Pio came to help sent by God to take over and protect us. Padre Pio was a Saint, Priest, Religious, Stigmatic, and Confessor.

He appeared and showed to Ron, the astrologist, his hand banded with the stigmata. Told him that he died in 1968 and that after he passed, he decided to help and continue to fight the devil on earth from the other side. He had to fight the devil himself all his life and received the stigmata. His hands were bleeding.

Then he showed Ron the vision of the last supper with the wine (blood) in one hand and the bread (body) in the other hand giving communion to CHADD.

He told VIE that he was now coming to help fight the devil for him. Padre Pio said that he came also to protect VIE from any harm, that he was her guide and her protector.

And that CHADD's mission was finished and came to completion, and he needed to be whole again, needed to rest of this life, be pure, be the being he was meant to be, and away from the suffering. That his time came to be happy now by saying:

"I just had to let now the energy of Padre Pio help me, and I left him my burden"

VIE had to rapidly dress to visit CHADD as he was still a patient at the behavior center to deliver the message.

She entered the place and had to wait. The time was flying by and the visitation time with it. Finally, CHADD arrived pushed by a nurse, and did not seem grounded. He was dehydrated and depleted of nutrients. He was looking pale and Grey, not shaved, smelling bad, uncleanly as he could not take a shower and was sweating, having a hard time breathing, and borderline delirious.

The psychiatric hospital removed his hydrating drops bottle, and he could only drink tap water when they would allow him. The more he was drinking from the fountain the more he was thirsty. VIE had to wait and try patiently for the right moment. She felt relieved when a few minutes before the end of the visitation she could rapidly deliver him Saint Padre Pio's message and give him his picture. CHADD in a quick gesture folded the paper and put it discretely in his pocket saying in a very low tone: VIE, listen, they have infiltrated a girl named Jazzy, it is the daughter of a General and a judge, they want me to marry her. You see what I mean? You marry her and you will be out soon? See the extortion once again, right? But you know that I love you and that we are already married. You are my Marie-Madeleine, and I am your blue flame. I know they do not believe that it is true, but it is better like this. We are the God Duo.

Chapter 29
Two Ghost Spies

I was busy getting ready to leave for an appointment at the office when I heard knocking at the front door.

Two young women introduced themselves as sisters.

Sisters: How are you doing today? We are here to see if we can help you.

VIE: Good morning, and nice to meet you sisters I am a Minister. Yes! You could help me by praying for my blue flame CHADD. Then I quickly narrated to them what he went through and what he was still going through and added

"It is still going on. Early morning, this past Friday, he insisted on driving the car that day. He started the car and at a fighting high speed, we entered the highway. He was passing by all cars, and it was obvious that he was not himself. I kept asking him to slow down but he was replying- let me drive I have been prepared to be a stuntman. I am a robot. It lasted all day until two suspicious Indian-looking policemen stopped us at gunpoint and drove him to Doctors Mr. and Mrs. Kalsam "IBEHAVE" behavioral Hospital. I kept telling them that we were both Ministers. I showed them my wallet-ordained Minister ID and told them that we were not violent, but they did not want to hear it. They called a tow company, had my car towed and they left me on the side of the road while disappearing with him in their car. Yes! Your prayers could help for sure"

The younger sister: Wow! This is quite a story!

The oldest: Let us pray then now

We prayed then they gave me a card and before leaving they wrote their private phone number as I asked them to. That evening I was guided to call the number and of course, the number was not in function.

CHADD was readmitted again to the "IBEHAVE" behavioral Hospital, and I received a phone call from him on the following Monday afternoon saying.

"Hurry and listen to me. I just passed in front of the Judge. Paul and Katrine are linked to the court. They seemed to have a high and tight connection with the justice system. They have issued a restraining order against you, and I am not supposed to talk to you. The judge wants me to go back to the asylum. Please bring me my personal belongings left in the car and do not call me anymore. I do not want you to be hurt"

What happened is that the secret government and his family know who we are and what mission we are here for. They do not want us to help humanity and they want to keep using him and make money with his stunts. So, they are separating us."

The younger sister: Wow! This is quite a story!

The oldest: Let us pray then now

We prayed then they gave me a card and before leaving they wrote their private phone number as I asked them to. That evening I was guided to call the number and of course, the number was not in function. It did not really surprise me, but I left a message and I never heard back from these "sisters."

I learned later through one of my spiritual guides that Katherine and Paul were pleased by the fact that we were not able to communicate anymore. And once again they manipulated his brain but against me. They got their grips on him again. Knowing by experience, that when it happens, he loses clarity of mind and has only once in a while a window of reality but quickly forgets. They know that he is unable to have correct judgment and I was not going that time to let them manipulate his brain against me and separate us again.

I decided to work from another dimension, and I asked for help from my Spiritual family on a much higher realm.

Chapter 30
Brainwashed and Programmed During Coma Finally Unveiled

While CHADD was in a Coma my physical body was here, but I was at the same time at his bedside from another realm. He was on life support, and I could observe that his, nurse in charge, kept putting on some headphones and repeatedly played again and again the same music, titles, songs, and specific groups.

I was wondering why, and I thought at that time that it was probably to keep him in a happy state of mind and that they did not have anything else to play. So, I did not have anything against it. It was much later on that I figured out what they did. They were programming his mind for their own purpose and entertainment agenda. A big industry and a great way to make a lot of money economically.

It did not click in my mind right away when he asked me for the first time to de-program him. It was much later and after a few events that I began to understand.

Of course! That is what they were doing. Using him and also controlling him then after.

His education was paid for by the Government mentor, the ticket offered him to see a well-known motivational man, the nurse in charge while he was in a coma that was introduced to before coma, the Factory outlet he was suggested by the same person from the Government to apply for a job and the co-worker girl that needed to find a free roof to stay, the handicapped girl living in a military camp he was guided to visit and they wanted him to marry, the world-famous studio he was also suggested to apply for a job as a stunt man, the world-famous also place for vacation and entertainment that infiltrated some insider and wanted him to sign a contract and changed the spelling of his name...the hotel he was guided to go to karaoke and to sing songs with famous singers from the groups he was listening again and again during his coma. The VIECH company car he was driving was out of control, the cameras everywhere filming him and where he was doubling some famous actors. The cars, offices, and phones bugged.

Most owners and managers of the entertainment industries are black government. What is this industry all about? Money? What for? Some answers were given to me in my dreams several months ago.

I saw the underground, prepared to shelter hundreds of thousands of people with many advanced technologies, that Human beings are unaware of and cannot even imagine, at least two hundred high-technology flying machines.

Clone beings living underground have built domes near ocean water underground where they can see outside from the inside and human beings that want to visit it must receive a shot that changes the DNA to be able to access the underground. The shot lasts only 20 minutes, DNA and physical changes occurring then cannot be reversed, so it's impossible to come back out and anyway alive. That is why only clones are inhabiting the underground.

What is funny is that Paul's son looked identical to CHADD at the same age as his daughter too!

All the entertainment money goes to build and maintain this underground. All funds from the entertainment industries, all movies done during events, or from cameras posted in public places, hospitals, and hotels ... all income goes to these underground projects.

Originally, planet Earth was Pleiadian. Some Angels fell and mixed with human beings with a different type of blood. Earth became a multi-pot and a human lab. Original strands of DNA were disconnected. Succeeded many years of atrocity. Human beings lost their connection to the ONE. Instead of acting from the heart center they acted from the emotional chakra. It is in dividing that they could better reign. It is how dark energies could so far keep people in fear. Many human beings could not support it anymore and some killed themselves. Today many are beginning to awaken but have no idea what they are looking for, how to get there, or what to do. They are sick and in pain, stressed, always working more trying to survive, and have less and less time to enjoy life and fall into depression and drugs. At the same time there are wars and fight and genocide and crimes all over the planet. Religious people are fighting in the name of God, and are killing in the name of God. But God is all of Love, God is of peace. God loves his children but unless you understand what is going on and call him, he cannot help you. You have to acknowledge him, love him, talk to him, and ask him. You do not need anybody for that he hears you. Simply turn yourself to your father and ask him for help.

God gave all of us freedom and are we not slaves? Slaves of who?

It is time to see the reality. You have been kept in the dark and we, CHADD & VIE went through all those traumas to help you.

Please see the reality. You are magnificent metaphysical beings that came on Earth to graduate. We are accessioning. Educate yourself, and seek him, not a religious group. He has never left you.

Chapter 31
VISION OF JUSTICE

We were heading towards the Natural grocery store. CHADD was driving when we heard the police siren. It took some time for CHADD and me to realize that it was for us. I told him to stop, and we pulled over rapidly. Before we even stopped the car, two policemen came in each side of the car pointing a gun at each of us at opposite front windows. One to my face and the other one to CHADD's face.

After witnessing every day in the news policemen shouting at people I was concerned and screamed:

Don't shoot! Don't shoot! We are not violent people we are both Ministers. Then I showed them my Minister ID, while CHADD was still silent his two hands visibly resting on the dashboard.

The Pakistan/American policeman on his side opened his door, and violently began to grab CHADD and pull him off his seat shouting: Get out, get out now! And he was beginning to handcuff CHADD who was half on his seat and halfway out of the car ready to fall on the road.

I again had to intervene and tell him, No! Please, officer, he is handicapped and cannot stand without support. He needs to support himself to the car plus it takes time for him to get out. Please he is handicapped. But the policeman was continuing to handcuff him.

Then I heard CHADD's voice saying: "Please, Police Officers, do not break my knees now. I already have my Achilles tendons cut, do not break my knees also."

Finally, the one at my window realized and went to take his wheelchair in the trunk of the car as I was begging him to do.

At the same time, the weather turned nasty with rain, wind, and thunderstorms.

My concern continued to grow when I saw now, the Policeman pushing CHADD in his wheelchair under the shade of a tree. Then came my turn, I was asked to sit in the mud on the side of the road under rain, wind, and thunderstorms. I was looking at my white cloth turning brown and felt the water through my cloth getting to my skin. I began to be very chilly, but I did not care. Cars were passing by us on the road.

Suddenly, I saw a towing company coming and backing up in front of the car ready to take the car away.

I was trying to understand but it did not make any sense to me. Unless... we were baker-acted.

Memory came back and rushed into my head of previous backer acting times.

Yes! So many. One time when he was sent to a behavioral center for a 72-hour evaluation it turned out two weeks!

He called me to come and visit him. When I went through the security a woman slowly approached me and with great precaution in a low voice told me" He was then baker acted by the police. This is why he is here. Now leave fast before he is in more trouble, and I left not knowing what to think.

But there is also another time that I remember quite well in detail. It was when he was admitted by Katherine to a mental hospital, and I happened to be visiting him during the visit of a middle-aged blond Psychiatric doctor and I heard her comment. "Hi, CHADD, do you remember me I was the doctor in charge many years ago, you were very young when Katherine admitted you for evaluation. It is obvious by now that psychiatric drugs do not work for you but what you need is a good psychologist to talk to. Someone you can talk about all you went through." There was also a nurse that known him for a long time and made the same type of comment: "You poor thing, no wonder you are here again, this is all you have seen and known all your life"

So, I am right he is baker-acted again. That is what it is once again, this is why Katherine got Paul to mislead my family and tried to convince them that I needed also to be evaluated and to try to trap me in psychiatric drugs. Like CHADD.

I returned my attention now to the scene. One out of the two police officers is taking charge. The second is still silent. The one taking charge, His look is weird, his eyes are looking weird too and his acts are bizarre. Why haven't we been asked for the registration of the car, why the policemen do not tell us the motive for stopping us?

I did not want my car to be towed and said to the Pakistan police man "Officer Kishore, this car is mine and I do not see the reason for my car to be towed" but Kishore remained silent. Then he approached me and said "Look! I am going to take CHADD to a hospital for evaluation, he has a mental problem and I do not want him to resist. Do not tell him anything and stay where you are. Do you hear me?"

The second Policeman came next to me while Kishore pushed CHADD into the police car.
A third police car joins the scene now. The policeman got out of the car. This one was taller with a bulletproof jacket. I thought that this was weirder by the minute. Why is he wearing bulletproof? And he told me "Get in the car NOW! and leave. GO! GO! Leave! You will hear from him in seventy-two hours."

Well! Three weeks later after a court "hearing" for a reason he is still trying to figure out, the ordained Minister and warrior of God CHADD, has been moved to another behavioral facility where he has been admitted and forced to ingest nine drugs at a time.

This bothered me a lot. I knew he was so close to being free. We have worked so hard for his freedom and now he was back to hell! I needed to understand and began to pray for clarity.

I was heard and last night one of my spiritual family visited me and took me to see. To have the entire truth on this situation on what happened and how it happened.

I first saw a man on the phone who was talking to Katherine.
"Hello! Katherine, How are you doing? Ok, I heard you. Yes. I agree we must do something. Do not worry I will take care of it. I will make sure he is

readmitted somewhere. Have a great day. I have it covered Katherine"

Then Mr. Bakiminn is making a phone call now:

"Forrest, Bakiminn speaking, you have CHADD's case in your courtroom soon, I have received a call from his family. His step-mom is very concerned. He is not ready to be released. He must be maintained on drugs, in one of these mental facilities under Carolinas control for at least ninety days. Thank you, Forrest. I know I can count on you."

Then Forrest is talking and Bakiminn again "Look! Have some appointed Guys stop him in the street somewhere, like we did in the past, it will take care of it all. It'll look normal."

Then I see myself now calling my cousin's defense attorney Brandy

"Hi Brandy, good morning. It is me VIE I need a favor from you. Can you pull CHADD's file tell me what is going on with his court case and call me back? Thanks.

Fifteen minutes later Brandy called me back" VIE, all I found is that he did not pay a ticket and his Driver's license is suspended. He needs to pay, and his driving license will be re-activated."

I turned towards my guides "This makes no sense or on the contrary, it makes all sense now. Wait a minute! Yes! It covers their acts and gives an excuse to the men in police uniforms to stop the car. They just have to use the fact that he was not long ago at the IBEHAVE place to re-admit him. Katherine has him once again away from me, on drugs, making me look mentally ill towards my family that she and Paul contacted. It is making my family think that she is a good-intentioned person who cares for him and Paul too. Wow, thanks for letting me view what happened" Once again we can witness a breach of the Fifth Amendment. The Fifth Amendment of the Constitution is not respected!

Then came another Court hearing. You will think that finally CHADD has been released.
Instead, here is the least of the drugs they force him to ingest:

Vistaril 25 MG (also used together with other medications given for anesthesia) Vistaril side effects hives; difficulty breathing; swelling of your face, lips, tongue, or throat. Restless muscle movements in your eyes, tongue, jaw, or neck; tremor (uncontrolled shaking); confusion; or seizure(convulsions). May include dizziness, drowsiness; blurred vision, dry mouth; or headache.

Norvasc (amlodipine) belongs to a group of drugs called calcium channel blockers.

Norvasc(5MG)side effects

- Hives; difficulty breathing; swelling of your face, lips, tongue, or throat. Call your doctor at once if you have a serious side effect such as: feeling like you might pass out; swelling in your hands, ankles, or feet pounding heartbeats or fluttering in your chest; or chest pain or heavy feeling, pain spreading to the arm or shoulder, nausea, sweating, general ill feeling.

Norvasc side effects may include headache; dizziness, drowsiness; tired feeling; stomach pain; or flushing (warmth, redness, or tingly feeling).

HCTZ 25 MG: dosage 9 am – 9 pm is for Edema (?)

Side effects:

- Hives; difficulty breathing; swelling of your face, lips, tongue, or throat. Stop using HCTZ and call your doctor at once if you have a serious side effect such as eye pain, vision problems; dry mouth, thirst, nausea, vomiting; feeling weak, drowsy, restless, or light-headed; fast or uneven heartbeat; muscle pain or weakness; numbness or tingly feeling; a red, blistering, peeling skin rash; or nausea, stomach pain, loss of appetite, low fever, dark urine, clay-colored stools, jaundice (yellowing of the skin or eyes).

HCTZ's other side effects may include:

- diarrhea; mild stomach pain; constipation; or blurred vision.
- Ativan 2MG, Lorazepam Intensol (by mouth)

Warning: This medicine can be habit-forming

Side effects:

- Depression, confusion, dizziness, clumsiness, unusual tiredness, thoughts of hurting yourself, severe drowsiness or weakness, slow heartbeat, trouble breathing

Cogentin/Benztropine 1mg
Warnings
This medicine may make you drowsy or cause you to have trouble thinking clearly and could affect you dangerously.
Possible side effects:

- With your neck muscles becoming stiff and suddenly weak. Jerky muscle movement you cannot control (often in the face, tongue, or jaw), trouble thinking, Bowel or stomach, heart problem. Allergic reaction: Itching or hives, swelling in your face or hands, swelling, or tingling in your mouth or throat, chest tightness, trouble breathing, confusion or extreme behavior changes, fast or uneven heartbeat, seeing or hearing things that are not real, severe constipation, or pain in your abdomen Severe dry mouth that causes trouble swallowing or speaking, loss of appetite, or weight loss Unable to sweat, or feeling overheated

Protonix (40mg)
Common Side Effects

- These side effects include insomnia, abdominal ache, diarrhea, burping, gas, hyperglycemia, nausea, throwing up, and skin rash.

Less Common Side Effects

- There are also some less common, but possible side effects of Protonix. These side effects include respiratory tract infection, coughing, constipation, chest ache, bronchitis, neck pain, backache, sore throat, anxiety, joint pain, dizziness, feeling lightheaded, indigestion, high levels of fat in the blood, migraine headache, flu syndrome, rhinitis, urinary tract infection (UTI), gastroenteritis and insufficient energy or strength.

Metropolol, Hypertensolol, Lopressor, Toprol XL, Toprol-XL

Side effects and warning

- Heart failure, blood vessel, asthma, heart failure, allergic reaction: Itching or hives, swelling in your face or hands, swelling, or tingling in your mouth or throat, chest tightness, trouble breathing, Lightheadedness, dizziness, or fainting, Slow heartbeat, Swelling in your hands, ankles, or feet, trouble breathing, tiredness, Worsening chest pain, Diarrhea, Mild dizziness, or tiredness.

Abilify

Increase suicidal thoughts or behaviors. Depression and other serious mental illnesses are themselves associated with an increase in the risk of suicide. Serious side effects may include:

- An increased risk of stroke and mini-stroke have been reported in clinical studies
- High fever, stiff muscles, confusion, sweating, and changes in pulse, heart rate, and blood pressure

may be signs of a condition called neuroleptic malignant syndrome (NMS), a rare and serious condition that can lead to death

- Increases in blood sugar levels (hyperglycemia) can happen in some people who take ABILIFY. Extremely high blood sugar can lead to coma or death.
- Changes in cholesterol and triglyceride (fat, also called lipids) levels in the blood have been seen in patients taking medicines like ABILIFY
- Weight gain has been reported in patients taking medicines like ABILIFY so your weight should be checked regularly
- ABILIFY and medicines like it have been associated with difficulty swallowing which may lead to aspiration or choking
- Uncontrollable movements of the face, tongue, or other parts of the body, as these may be signs of a serious condition called tardive dyskinesia (TD). TD may not go away, even if you stop taking ABILIFY. TD may also start after you stop taking ABILIFY
- Orthostatic hypotension (decreased blood pressure) or lightheadedness or fainting when rising too quickly from a sitting or lying position has been reported with ABILIFY
- Decreases in white blood cells (WBC; infection-fighting cells) have been reported in some patients taking ABILIFY. Patients with a history of a significant decrease in WBC count or who have experienced a low WBC count due to drug therapy should have their blood tested and monitored during the first few months of therapy

- Seizures (convulsions) have been reported with ABILIFY. Tell your healthcare provider if you have a history of or are at risk for seizures
- ABILIFY and medicines like it can affect your judgment, thinking, or motor skills. You should not drive or operate hazardous machinery until you know how ABILIFY affects you
- Medicines like ABILIFY (aripiprazole) can impact your body's ability to reduce body temperature; you should avoid overheating and dehydration.

Though CHADD was in Abilify side effects he remembers seeing the same Court Magistrate that was next room in the hotel he was in.

She told CHADD" Just let the door close slowly" and was also behind the front desk. The court Magistrate was now the nurse giving him his medication in the State hospital where he had been admitted.

Not only this was weird, but a Girl named Michaella admitted herself and asked him for his Social Security and Phone number begging him to marry him offering him his body, and showing him his private parts inside the State facility. I found out later that she was an actress.

Another girl was given an overdose of Abilify, her heart stopped beating. She was moved out and transferred to an emergency room where she was declared dead, and a month later CHADD found out that three other patients had been killed by overdosing on pills or drug injections.

Chapter 32
CHADD is Denied of the Right to a Fair Trial

CHADD was never brought to court though the court date was rescheduled. Two women testified against him that he did not even know, and there was no defense counsel to defend him. But Katherine, the archon, was in court.

After CHADD left the room where the Indian doctors were he entered another room still inside the mental hospital where Katherine, Caroline, Jo, and a social worker were all reunited. This was supposed to be the official trial in Court.

Caroline spoke and said, I am going to make an investigation on VIE and we will set something up to baker act her and put her in jail. CHADD you must never talk to this woman ever again.

Three days later Katherine called him and told CHADD that he would be admitted into a State mental hospital hours away from his hometown for six months. I thought how did she know?

The following Tuesday I was awakened by an Angelic voice: "Good morning VIE, I am Pierre your ancestor. VIE be prepared CHADD was asked to sign his admission into a mental Hospital in "Utrapt County" up North this morning, he refused, and the nurse named KIO committed a forgery, she signed for him. She told him ironically that he was going to start a new life. It is all about Insurance making big money on him and separating you both. It's been years that they are making money on him, with the cooperation of Katherine and the legal system. This trial is illegal, and he did not have any lawyer of course to defend him. So, CHADD has been found competent but did not have the right to a fair trial. You are right VIE; the CHADD case is a breach of the Fifth Amendment to the Constitution. Also, Katherine went with Carlos, here is Carlos in the scenario again, to visit CHADD the day before and they bought him new clothes, they knew that CHADD was going to be transferred today for six months. Katherine wants him back in the house to continue to use and torture him. He never made a complaint, but he has been abused and beaten by her for many years many times in his wheelchair. CHADD must request a change of Judge and attorney and should have his mother not allowed in the courtroom if it was possible. Which should be now that all is going to be unveiled.

But here is the way Carolina told VIE:

"When I looked at the court legal papers I understood that something was not right. How can CHADD, competent by the court, still under my guardianship be sentenced to go to a hospital up north? I opened an investigation the same day and agreed to CHADD requests and asked for a new trial"

CHADD on his side answered the questioning and finally got it all out of his chest. For the first time in years, he told the truth about Katherine and Paul's abuses. He gave Katherine thirty-five of his life to protect his step-mom, and the opportunity to change, but all she cared about was money and Paul did not want to change his attitude either. So, he gave up on them and decided to turn the page. He had to, he could not continue he gave them thirty-five years of forgiveness and the option to change many, many times.

Is Carolina part of them? She kept telling him to get along with his stepmother and confessed to me that Katherine was the one in power!

AND THE TRUTH HAVE SET US FREE!

Chapter 33
A Golden Age and Cosmic Evolution Dance

Wavoka the Christ came first to the white man and was killed for trouble.

Waneka the Messiah said that he would return and had. In Nevada, then migrated and spread his word to the lands west of Blackfoot.

And Waneka the Messiah said:

"I have sent for you, and I am glad to see you. Today is the time to teach you to dance. I want you to dance the Golden Age of our Cosmic dance of evolution when everyone has a high frequency of light of a higher dimension, that of angels and light beings. The dance where you shine with pure light and joyously live in the moment and also sing sacred songs. It is a regenerative continuity between life and death, a prayer for life, world renewal, and thanksgiving. The bad spirits are taken into the prop and then cast into the wind. You will be purified by the dance, and you will re-enter the world refreshed and regenerated."

It is time for you to witness the cosmic nativity of another world coming. The rising sun connects with the birth of the divine son. It will crush out everything old and dying and those who are in peace in their heart are in great shelter of life, but like I told you, there is no shelter for evil.

The ceremony will cause many of you to collapse and enter in trance, it will be followed by a vision, similar to what happens on a vision quest, only here many of you will be given guidance for the good of all of you. You will see and speak to your relatives. In a sense, this is a community vision quest to renew the people and the bioregion.

Many will be healed by the goose medicine. It will appear in a V formation indicating that one is not stuck in old patterns that need changing. Receiving Goose medicine is to carry the energy of the journey of the great quest, to set a high goal, and to find the right ways to navigate towards it. It teaches you how to navigate the greatest turbulence in lives as well as how to make greater headway when things are going well.

It is the return of the old-time life and your recognition. Faithful dancing, clean living, peaceful adjustments with everyone, and following God's chosen leaders will hasten the resurrection of dead relatives and the restoration of days of your prosperity.

The third order is under the domination of a Greek goddess (the third archon) of the underworld and has blocked the power of the true Trinity, but through the new opening of Melchizedek the region of the Goddess falls. The power of darkness is cast down by the sword of Orion, or Osiris, who eliminates the black smoke of war and death through higher knowledge and greater music that takes hold to transform the powers of the sun and the stars. Gates open for the new arrival of celestial intelligence, and we can work in harmony and unity. While a higher Love and Divine order come in instead.

Melchizedek is sent to humanity at the time of the second Coming of Christ which will come during the time of Cosmic Change and the Cosmic dance of evolution taught by Waneka.

Melchizedek order works with Archangels Michael and Archangels Gabriel who direct the outpouring of Light into parts of Chaos wherever it is needed, and the powers of the Trinity manifest together to emanate Light into space in all directions and mysteriously transform the regions.

Wavoka is showing us that we must reach beyond the stars to receive and bring forth Light.

The third archon is one of many entities representing darkness and associated with sorcery and she is the deception at the interdimensional crossroads. Her purpose is to destroy humanity and she has many arch-demons under her command who entered humanity and bring them to falsehoods and lies. And cause them to lust after that which is not theirs. And the souls that she steals away, she turns them over to her arch-demons under her command so that they may torment them in her dark smoke before to are destroyed.

It is by breaking through the fourth dimension of time (our linear time dimension) the third archon (the Greek goddess) and also the Typhon and understanding his power, that we will begin to inherit the eternal tree of life.

The third archon is worshiped by the pagans at solstice and the VAJRA has been taken away to be used, at solstice for an ultimate battle.

Although the philosophical systems of Buddhism and Christianity have evolved in rather different ways, the moral precepts advocated by Buddhism have some similarities with the Christian moral precepts developed more than two centuries later: respect for life, respect for the weak, rejection of violence, and pardon to sinners and tolerance.

The main Greek cities of the Middle East happen to have played a key role in the development of Christianity, such as Antioch and especially Alexandria, and "it was later in this very place that some of the most active centers of Christianity were established"

Khronos (primeval god) was represented in the Greco-Roman mosaic as Aion, "eternity" personified. He stands against the sky holding a wheel inscribed with the signs of the zodiac. Beneath his feet, Gaia (Mother Earth) is usually seen reclining. Aion is described as an old man with long white hair and a beard. Mosaics, however, present a youthful figure.

The Queen of the Underworld "Persephone" was carried off the land of the Dead. The excavated Amphipolis tomb mosaic depicts the figure of the goddess Persephone, queen of the Underworld (abducted by Pluto). Identified as Persephone, daughter of Zeus, the goddess portrayed on a mosaic floor provides a key new clue on who was laid to rest in the immense, marble-walled tomb 61 miles (99 kilometers) northeast of the Greek city of Thessaloniki. The image of Persephone closely resembles one in a painting from the royal cemetery of Vergina, where Alexander the Great's father was buried. The mosaic shows the abduction of Persephone by Pluto. Persephone mosaic as they cleared the floor of one of the tomb's inner chambers. The tomb might hold the remains of Roxane, Alexander the Great's wife, or Olympias, his mother. Both women were put to death by one of Alexander's generals, Cassander, as he secured the throne of ancient Macedonia.

Carried Off to the Land of the Dead. Hades, the god of the underworld, spied on Persephone, the daughter of Zeus and the harvest goddess, working in a field, and decided to make her his wife. So, he captured her and took her to the underworld, where she became his queen. The mosaic portrays Hades as a bearded charioteer carrying off the curly-haired Persephone, who looks back wistfully toward her home. Running in front of the chariot is a third figure, the messenger god Hermes, who wears a scarlet cloak and hat and a pair of winged sandals as he leads the way to the underworld.

Crystals of Green honor Persephone, the Greek Goddess of Spring. She represents celebration and the Earth alive with new growth.

Moldavite may also be used to honor Gaia, the Greek Earth Mother Goddess. Born directly out of Chaos, the primal emptiness, she was the first (or one of the first) beings to appear during the process of creation and is honored as being the Earth itself.

A crystal from a ship from the heavens, Moldavite the stone born of the stars, the "fire pearl" and the Stone of Shambhala, the most sacred jewel of Tibet believed, of celestial origin, from the constellation of

Orion, and further asserted it must be the same stone as in the Holy Grail. Moldavite, associated with the phoenix, consumed by fire and reborn in fire is a symbol of transfiguration and spiritual renewal.

Dating even into pre-history, Moldavite has always been revered as a spiritual talisman and an amulet for good fortune and fertility. The Neolithic peoples of Eastern Europe wore Moldavite at least 25,000 years ago, and the earliest known goddess statue, the famed Venus of Willendorf, was discovered in a digging site with several Moldavite amulets. In some versions, the Grail was the chalice used by Christ at the Last Supper, while others believed the Grail was not a cup but a stone that fell from the sky during the war between God and Satan and was brought to earth by angels who remained neutral.

In history, an actual "Grail" a bowl, called the Saint Graal reputed to be a platter used by Christ at the Last Supper, was discovered, and brought to Napoleon. Napoleon, under expert examination, was disappointed to find it was made of green glass. While Moldavite is green glass, there is only speculation as to whether the true bowl might have been substituted to keep it from Napoleon, or whether the bowl was indeed the Grail.

Another historically noted chalice made of gold and adorned with Moldavites was used as an ostensory (a vessel in which the consecrated Host is presented for the veneration of the faithful) and was passed down through the centuries but disappeared during the Second World War.

In the last century, Moldavite has found acclaim as a spiritual relic associated with the legends of the Holy Grail. In recorded history, the Grail vessel was held to be the cup that caught the blood of Christ as He died on the cross. In the Arthurian romances, the Grail cup magically passed among the knights and ladies seated at the Round Table during the feast of Pentecost, giving each the food they most desired - holy nourishment. A drink from the Grail brought healing and rejuvenation, and a spiritual awakening. It guided the knights on quests for their right paths of destiny. Moldavite is the Grail of alchemists, the Philosopher's Stone, for its qualities of transformation and the bestowal of youth and longevity, the green stones from the sky wearied as amulets.

Throughout the Middle Ages Moldavite was so highly prized only nobility or royalty were allowed to wear it, it was believed to bring good luck and harmony. Many specimens reside in various museums and institutions, private collections, and even NASA possesses several Moldavites. The Swiss government gave a gift of Moldavite to Queen Elizabeth II on the tenth anniversary of her coronation, a beautiful naturally sculpted raw stone set in platinum and surrounded by diamonds and black pearls. There was also a rosary of faceted Moldavite beads with a carved Madonna made for Pope John Paul II as a gift from the Czechoslovakian people.

Chapter 34
Matrix or the Illusion That Blocks You In

A few days after that I heard the story about the moldavite stone, I was offered one beautiful moldavite ring mounted with diamonds on the band. After a rather busy morning, I lay on my bed in the early afternoon, tired and wanting to sleep.

I fell into a lucid dream about the new ring on my finger.

A sudden energetic push, tangibly felt in my back in the heart region, catapults me into another realm. I was suddenly in an altered state of consciousness somewhere else. New chambers of consciousness are opening. My body is involved, he is flooded with currents of light and colors with new information. The frequency changes with the quality of consciousness and I am pushed into another higher realm. I am now in another form of beingness.

I am still in a body; it is pure energy although it is different. The ancient Matrix is not there anymore with a complete sensation of freedom with a new rhythmic interval of experience and expansion of myself.

I know that this is not a personal experience but of a completely different nature. It has nothing to do with myself, my own body, yet light and energy might be rushing through it which expands. It has to do with substance, with the transformation of matter and its consciousness.

And I know that it is a new vibrational and transformational frequency that is causing a shift in the global consciousness in which the body is involved. I just was tuning into this new reality.

As I continued in this lucid dreaming of the new world I had a strong desire to remain here. I do not want to go back to the world of limitations. I strongly want to go home with my physical body.

Then I fall deeply asleep.

Saint Agnes appears she stay at a small distance. (Patron Saint of engaged couples) She says now "I am known as Saint Agnes, but I am now Agni Spritu. I am not in a body now. I am an Angel, but I can be addressed by either name. You have asked to work with Saint Hildegard, but you must work with me also. It's trinity and it is time now to work with (women-female) and always address first women"

My awareness is different now, the space between things is full and there is stillness. I understand that we are in this space. I understand now that the matrix that we are is in truth free. It is the infinite Source Field and our Consciousness.

The matrix is the illusion that we are locked in. Only those who are aware, are already being released from this bondage as the universal new frequencies have already set humanity free. We are eternally free and expanded in unison with the space of primordial matter in which all things arise. It is an artificial world initiated by the secret government (black government) to keep human beings trapped in their agenda. They are using advanced technology to create that illusionary world using people's minds. I understand that we will continue in this matrix world as long as it still exists, as the enormous majority of mankind is still bound by it through its belief. It is up to each single one of us to tune in and accept this new Conscious Awareness because until then the old world continues.

Chapter 35
The Asian Couple from Calcutta

The first medallion found in the cave on Indian land (receiving the coming of Christ) represents the matter, Christ established on Earth when the Spirit of Jesus descended into the matter. The second medallion found in Antioch, the Fire symbol (Merkabah- Chariot Mysticism) announces the second coming of spirit and the (ascension time)

VIE VAJRA, used as the representation of our intellect that brings our liberation, is the most powerful tool for striking the dark energies like any other kind of self-defense. It is a thunderbolt diamond used by VIE hands to strike the devil. The VAJRA was passed through the generation of the Buddha's bloodline and was recorded back in 326 BC when Alexander the Great invaded India. Monks in the monastery, where it was kept safe, benefited from it a lot against their opponents.

But the Asian couple that robbed VIE went back home to Calcutta and brought with them the VAJRA to be part of an ancient pagan ritual.

The Thuggee, tuggee, also called (thugna means to deceive or Phansigar) is an organized gang of professional assassins. The Thugs traveled in groups across India for six hundred years. Although the Thugs traced their origin to seven Muslim tribes, Hindus appear to have been associated with them at an early period. The Thugs would join travelers and gain their confidence. This would allow them to then surprise and strangle their victims by pulling a handkerchief or noose tight around their necks. They would then rob their victims of valuables and bury their bodies. This led them to also be called Phansigar, a term more commonly used in southern India. The Thuggee had their female counterparts in a secret sect of Tantrists who held that it was only by a constant indulgence in passion that a human could ever achieve total union with Kali. Only indulgence in the five vices that corrupt the soul of humankind: wine, meat, fish, mystical gesticulations, and sexual indulgence, could drive the poisons out of the human body and purify their souls. They had a peculiar code of ethics whose rules forbade the killing of fakirs, musicians, dancers, sweepers, oil vendors, carpenters, blacksmiths, maimed or leprous persons, Ganges water-carriers, and women. Despite the restriction against the murder of females, however, the presence of wives traveling with their husbands often necessitated the strangling of a woman to protect the secrecy of society. The murderous craft of the Thuggee was hereditary. Its practitioners were trained from earliest childhood to murder by the quick, quiet method of a strong cloth noose tightened about the neck of their victims. This weapon, the "Rumal," was worn knotted about the waist of each member of the Thuggee. Their extreme secrecy combined with their mastery of murder made the Thugs the deadliest secret society in all of history. A secret cult of murderers roaming India goes back at least as far as the 13th century.

They were first mentioned dated around 1356. In the 1830s they were targeted for eradication by William Bentinck and his chief captain William Henry Sleeman. They were seemingly destroyed by this effort.

The term Thuggee is derived from the Hindi word "thug" which means "thief". Related words are the verb thug, "to deceive", from the Sanskrit saga "fraudulent", and from tathagata "he conceals". This term for a particular kind of murder and robbery of travelers is popular in South Asia and particularly in India.

A South Asian couple Thuggee was sent to the United States with the mission to find the Key to the universe, rob the VAJRA from VIE, and bring it back to Calcutta.

They went first to California. They landed in Los Angeles. Dr. Singh member of the Thuggee cult was waiting for them. That first night they talked very late about the plan to find VIE.

The next morning, they contacted the Indian thuggees' doctors community and were told that their next meeting would take place the following Monday and invited me to join them. Monday came and they took a bus that dropped them not very far, 10 minutes' walk, from the location. The building was an old and closed building in the back of a dark alley in a park with nothing else around. But when they approached the building they could see that some candles were burning in one of the rooms. They pushed the entrance door and took the hallway towards the room with candles. They found about fifty Thuggees sitting on the floor on their little rug in a yogi position. The meeting lasted late until early morning, and they were told to travel to San Diego and meet with Dr. Vangali.

After a few hours of sleep, they took a bus to meet Vangali. They had to wait until late at night when Vangali finished his shift at the hospital. Again, long hours of discussion took effect but not much came from it. They had no clue how to find this Key. Dr. Vangali suggested then that they travel to San Francisco and meet his friend Dr. Gandam as he had many connections there and also in Florida.

A few days later they met with the Psychiatric Dr. Gandam and another Dr. in Psychology. The psychologist told them that they should research in Florida. He heard something about someone who was seen at a Qigong convention with something unusual around her neck. He was an Indian psychiatric doctor who worked in a state hospital. This Indian acquaintance doctor also saw the same person wearing it at a convention presenting some Qi- Light.

The Asian Couple from Calcutta decided to stay overnight before leaving. They needed to find out where the bus station was. Early morning, they used the computer in the lobby of a hotel to locate the bus station and their way to get there. Preferably walking as it would be less expensive. Luckily they were only a 20-minute walk from it but the bus was not leaving before 5 hours. They took a little walk around to kill the time and finally got on the bus to Miami. But while they were walking around they met an Indian man. The Indian man confirmed seeing a woman also with something quite unusual around her neck with very strong energy coming from it. She seemed to be with a lot of people around and he was wondering if it was because of the unusual object around her neck. The Asian couple stared at each other; they knew they were on the right track. The Key would be theirs soon.

They rapidly thanked the man and headed towards a phone and called the cult organization in Calcutta. The Thuggees in Calcutta were very happy and told them to go to the Acid Rock hotel, where they had made a reservation for a few days there. They were instructed to make sure to leave the hotel as soon as they had the key in their possession and fly back to Calcutta.

They went straight in a cab from the bus to their hotel where two Indian doctors were already waiting for them. The doctors asked them if they could go to their room to have a private meeting. They had important information to share.

The oldest doctor began to say "We are aware by the organization of your important mission. We have decided. It is going to take place tonight. You are looking for a woman, she will come with a man in a wheelchair. You will give this to the waitress to put in her drink. It's a drug that will last until tomorrow morning. The man is in a wheelchair and will act a little bit crazy. We have given him a drug and manipulated his brain making him act crazy and he will not have clarity of mind and no recollection. The woman will look like she is drunk, and nobody will suspect you. Our association works with mental hospitals and behavioral facilities, and we have a strong relationship with many different authorities. The man and the woman will both act weird, and the hotel will call the Sheriff. Do not worry, all will be covered and taken care of. Your room is paid just leave the hotel to catch your plane as soon as CHADD & VIE are arrested. If you have to wait too long for your connection take a bus and catch your plane from Georgia.

We will meet you upon landing in Calcutta.

Chapter 36
The Armageddon

The Armageddon is the last battle between good and evil before the Day of Judgment. The place where the last battle between good and evil will be fought. Armageddon is a biblical term directly associated with the Second Coming of Christ.

The battle of Armageddon refers to the final war between human Governments and God. These Governments and their supporters oppose God even now by refusing his ruler-ship.

The battle of Armageddon will bring human ruler-ship to an end.

It is the time which ends the reign of the false prophets, the idols that we call "celebrities". It is the time when the network of the elite is overthrown, dynastic families of wealth and privilege of those who have run this world since the dawn of civilization, to their maximum advantage and the extreme detriment of the people. It is the end of their tricks and tactics to keep enriching themselves at the people's expense.

It is the time when we recover our divine inheritance, what is ours by divine right.
It is the time of awakening and remembering
Jesus Christ will lead a heavenly army to victory over God's enemies

Chapter 37
The Attempting Murder by Poison

There I am lying down on my long comfortable chair on the sand, under the shadow of the trees cradled by the sound of the waves and the warm caress of the sun on my skin that made me fall asleep.

I am now in great peace and harmony reunited with all members of my Spiritual family far away from Gaia.

All is so brilliant, pure, and vivid. All is so clear and unpolluted. I can hear the peacock in the background and the birds. The Tibetan Monks are toning, and it makes my heart happy. Every one of my guides and my ancestors are excited and want to talk to me at the same time. I have to ask them to gently take turns as I want to hear it all.

My great, great, great ancestor Athenais is speaking first:

You know that Carlos is with the Mafia and part of the deal. Justice self-appointed has a piece of CHADD's monthly Government checks, and Carlos is, like Katherine (his stepmother) and Caroline. They all split his money while he is in a Concentration Camp for Catholics, the asylum. CHADD was deprived of a fair trial because they were not expecting you, VIE, and him to team up and resist for so long.

At the same time I heard this beautiful song in Latin and saw some Monks singing "...Tu Spiritutue!

Amennn, HOooo, HOooo, Amennn...nnn, Amennn..."

My ancestor Louis is taking turns now:

The Indian cult and thuggery that took your VAJRA have used it to hypnotize you and access your brain. Ascended Master Faith is going to talk to the reporter. They will dematerialize the VAJRA and get it back to you in a safe place. The diamond ring that has been stolen in your office will be attached to the chain.

Pierre Montour de la Roue now:

As Athenais was telling you they did not expect you to resist and battle them for such a long time, and their only alternative they concluded, is to separate you both.

Athenais again:

When CHADD was born, like every baby, his power, soul, and spirit were weak because of the burden of forgetfulness that is heavy on planet Earth. Its consciousness was cut off from the higher worlds and he ate from the substance of the world of the archons, his stepmother Katherine.

The archons are the ruling forces of non-physical intelligence which seek to control the
Experiments of life are present in the thirteen eons and chaos. Remember that Katherine was sitting on his bedside when he was asleep and was whispering in his ears and imprinting the evil world's way.

Here was his body existing in ignorance and misguided, a soul that was torn between the

Higher power and the force of the archon (the counterfeiting spirit). Katherine began the process of teaching his soul how to long for things of the earth. Causing his soul to reflect upon things of the earth during the night cycle when it should be participating consciously in the spiritual realms. Later on with drugs alternating their consciousness also during his sleep.

Jesus spoke of how the soul comes into the body, and yet it is the soul that guides the body and chooses the direction it will take along the path. This is where Free Will comes into play, for the soul chose the power either of the Light or of the counterfeiting spirit.

Later on, Katherine seeing you re-entering his life, used the power of her marital union with his father and used his father against him. Then when his father got weak with his illness, she kept him alive sucking his energy, and used Paul her son at that time, to attack to weaken you. Archons feed themselves with others' energy not food like human beings.

Now they all work together, Marco, Katherine and Paul, and Caroline back and forth, with the dark Government, these archons that elected themselves in key places everywhere, to separate you and him. It is part of the Armageddon battle. They fear your connection and your power. They have seen what you have been able to achieve with CHADD and would not like to lose their grip on him. He is a big asset for them. They would not like to have to say he was a big asset to us.

Ancestor Louis:

I am Louis also call "le Roi soleil". So CHADD was deprived of a fair trial and sent to an asylum, hoping that he would finally give up. But he did not. They first injected him with allergic substances, plus two vaccination shots at the same time, and added many drugs in pills, up to eleven three times a day, and finally one night while he was sleeping, the state official self-appointed, infiltrated a "nurse archon" to poison him.

Half asleep he saw her hugging him and heard her say with her metallic voice that she loved him and while her dark archon eyes were rolling she injected him with poison. He was under an Ambien sleeping drug pill that he was forced to ingest to induce sleep and could not react or defend himself. His sleep was heavy.

He began with what he thought was flu symptoms. A terrible headache and was given some Tylenol, then diarrhea, blood appeared in his tools, and his nose bled. The doctor told him that nothing was wrong with his body and that he would get better soon. CHADD began to throw up blood and it never stopped for the entire night. He felt weak and went to bed. It seems that nothing was left in energy in his physical body. ·

But they have no power over the carbon-based physical body.

"I called the next morning to talk to him as usual and I was told by a man that he was sick all night and was moved early morning somewhere else, but no one knew where and the man hung up the phone. I called again and heard: This is the United Nations, I have the book and the cross, stop calling here. Then the man hung up the phone as the previous person had.

The reference to the book and the Cross is the Catholic Student Bible study and the cross I mailed him. The logo CHADD & VIE is printed on the first page of the book and is preceded by a handwritten note "To my husband,...." Marie- Madeleine.

My mailed package had been in trouble or never reached its point. He had to wait 10 days before they gave it to him, though it was delivered on time. It was guaranteed no later than 2 days by 4 pm and it has been delivered as scheduled. He kept asking for his mail and was noted as a difficult patient and he was told that he would be retained in place longer.

I finally, after a third phone call, could get some information on where he had been

Transferred. I was connected that time to a nurse who told me that his bed was being made and to call back 20 minutes later, which I did. I had a nurse named Amandine who gave me a quick statement on his health and was going to also hang up the phone on me. I argued a little bit with her, and she finally put him on the phone. He was on I-V and his voice was not very reassuring. I decided not to put any negative thoughts into it and wished him to get well soon and to rest as much as he could.

The following morning, I called by breakfast time, and he answered. His voice was much better, and he told me that the Doctor officially recognized that he had been poisoned. But CHADD was very down by the vision of all that was going on around him. One person was trapped in a chair, I could hear some incoherent language, and some were moaning in terrible pain that would never ease. I had in a split second the image of what hell could be and felt bad about what he was going through. And I began to pray.

Athenais:

VIE, we are part of a long-line family of Christians. Our family has continued the tradition until that day of ordained Nuns and Priests members and, the celebration of an office by our family members and Priests before all family reunions, the annual "cousin". Our children, as you have been, all been baptized by our family Priests and when it was possible in our private Churches.

This was part of what they decided to do two thousand years ago for two thousand years, which is now the end. It is now the Armageddon time.

When you wrote to the Priest at the Diocese he did not believe you. Nowadays Catholics do not believe in reincarnation anymore. They still do not admit the reincarnation, though they have the truth written in their original prints in the Vatican Library, but no one consults it.

It is why you have been guided by us to write and send a text to the Priest again, to inform him that you tried to attract the attention of the Diocese before he was poisoned. Now they have the evidence. It is in their hands. Remember that the deceased Paul John Paul the Second said that he was working on it not a very long time ago. That he was going to talk to the newly elected Pope Francis.

VIE, your time is coming for both of you. You are called Lady Liberty and Justice. Your name means life/ankh, and the ankh inscriptions mean forever and ever, as you know you have been chosen to be the door to the Divine. You belong to the Lord. You are Victory and both CHADD and you are Victorious in Christ. It is inevitable. Failure is not an option. You will be reunited with your husband soon, very soon. One, Oneness.

The next morning, I got CHADD on the phone and he greeted me with the "I feel great today,
I am still on a liquid diet, and I have lost about seventeen pounds in five days but I cannot wait to get busy. I have so much work waiting for me" I have written another song and I have so much energy going through my body now, but I need you to hold my hand when I sing.

The same night he was transferred back to the unit where he had been poisoned. He recognized the blond archon nurse who greeted him with" Do you feel better now?" And she ordered him to ingest the numerous pills again. He looked at her and said: No, thank you I do not feel very good tonight and he went to bed. At midnight he was awakened and offered again the pills. He rolled himself on his other side and said nothing. The nurse did not insist and left.

Wednesday morning, I was on the phone with him, and someone came and interrupted our conversation. I heard him say thank you, Father. It was a priest, his new roommate who was given an envelope. Inside was his cross. Then I had a new vision and was able to connect the dots and had full clarity of the situation: I saw that Carolina was paid not to help his case by the judge and one person in the head center. An individual who has been assigned to CHADD's case made a deal with Katherine. When he sees someone helping in a CHADD case he fires the person, like CHADD's Lawyer, before he was assigned a public defender. Carolina accepted when he was in transition between drugs and detox. She accepted as she thought "Well! He is taking drugs why not accept the money"

Now I am observing another scene. I see Katherine she is at his bank, she is with Carlos, and talking to the manager. They have closed the door for a private meeting. I sneak inside to hear what they say.

Katherine is speaking: "You will get a percentage of course every month for helping us. My poor step-son is now in an Asylum. He had a head injury in the past. I need to pay his bills and his friend is here with me today, she was referring to Carlos, who is helping me with all the administration and paperwork. But the only way to access his account cannot be done without your cooperation and of course your discretion."

Now Carlos and Katherine left the bank deal, they are driving towards the Social Security office, she needs to also make a bank account transfer for the remaining half amount from the monthly Social Security.

By the end of the day, they had transferred the other half of the CHADD Government check. It will be going to a "family" bank account that only Katerine and Carlos have access to.

"Now! CHADD has nothing left to live when he'll be released from the Asylum. This was his only freedom!" said Katherine -now it makes all sense. I see Katherine and she is splitting all of CHADD's money between the managers of the bank, the Court one head assigned man, the judge, the bank manager, Carlos, Paul, and her. I cannot believe what I am seeing!

They are all corrupt. At the social security place, it was easy, and quickly done as she had been his guardian before he became his guardian. The employee knew her. CHADD had never received the total amount of his check and has been lied to since he became handicapped since he has been entitled to a Government check.

She originally set up two accounts and he never knew the amount Social Security paid him each month. She was getting, half of his check posted in a bank out of the state in her name since she self-elected herself his guardian, and Katherine was taking mostly all the remaining from the other bank account directly from him for payment of his room. He was left all these years with just enough to pay himself for a few cups of coffee.

They are all corrupted and greedy, and to be able to continue stealing from him he was by the Court Ordered in asylums. I called CHADD to inform him of my visions and he took the decision right to the judge and to send a copy to the International Criminal Court of Law.

He asked the priest, the chaplain, if he would be willing to type a letter for him that he would then sign and mail with copies to some different people for his and my protection, in the country and overseas.

Chapter 38
CHADD's Letter to the Court

Your Honor, since my earliest age, since kindergarten and before I could learn my rights, the system decided to label me and put me on prescribed psychiatric drugs and my life became hell. If you haven't ever been put on psychiatric drugs I would like to explain what I mean by living in hell. I began to sweat, I had horrible nightmares, my heart beating abnormally fast, I could not think clearly anymore, and every time that I asked for a reduction at least of the dosage it would instead increase. I fell into a coma by the end of my teenage, due to drugs. While I was in a coma I was still conscious of my surroundings, and I saw four medical female doctors working together to dislocate my hip. What was this for? This was not the end, I was awakening from a coma when for no medical reason again, my Achilles tendons were severed. Unless that was due to incompetency.
Then I had a heart attack due also to prescription drugs. Yes, due to side effects and I am attaching with this letter the list of all the meds I had to ingest and their side effects for you to review.

You see your honor, side effects go from heart attacks, heavy sweats, abnormally heart beating, a foggy state of mind, loss of memory...to suicidal thoughts. I became from that day on handicapped in a wheelchair, an athlete, and followed a life of numerous backing acts between my family, the system, the sheriff, police, and doctors with the

Conspiracy of the health insurance and the mental hospitals, behavioral hospitals then finally asylums. Why such a hard on me all these years?

I have been brutalized, tortured, beaten, stigmatized, and shot against my will with 18 gage needles of vaccinations and drugs, to which no one could have ignored that I was allergic, it was noted in my file. I had a heart attack that luckily I survived but was still not released from drugs.

I was poisoned, by an overdose of medications, passed on the floor, and woke up with black eyes due to the overdose of medications my stomach had to be pumped, I had to be under I-V and on a liquid diet also due to a prescriptions overdose of psychiatric drugs and by drops in my foods and all that happened while I was admitted without my consent, and court-ordered, under psychiatric drugs in the last asylum I am. In these places, the court sent me I have received psychedelic and psychotropic shots in an attempt to restrain me from writing the lyrics of my songs! Someone does not want me to write any songs. Are they scared that the truth would get out through the music and my songs? Or were they trying to make me change my lyrics?

I have been deprived of all my rights, and forced to ingest dangerous drugs. My monthly Government check has been taken from my bank account without my consent or signature!!! While I had to live in asylums, one infested with rats as big as an opossum...

With all due respect, your honor, enough is enough, I am asking for reparation and retribution. I am asking the court for compensation for the deprivation of my freedom, my rights, the right to a fair trial, the destruction of my life, and the deprivation of character.

I have a history in file of mental illness, no income, no car, no phone, etc. Nothing. I do not exist.

The court knows very well that I am not violent, and I have never hurt anybody, though the system has tried hard, I was forced to be on psychedelic and psychotropic drugs.

I have never killed, beaten, bruised, kicked, or poisoned anybody and I am asking the court for repair for the damages. My money has been stolen, and my life was past battling to survive, and not become insane, in these mental institutions in which I have been sent by the system that has failed me.

End of last year I had a "trial" date, but I was never brought to court. Instead, I went in front of a meeting in the hospital I was in. That was a mock court trial. I found myself in front of the hospital Doctor, the social worker from the place, another from another behavioral hospital, and my father's wife (Katherine) I had no lawyer to defend me but a verdict! I was moved to another behavioral center for about 14 days, for evaluation they said, then to an asylum! For the second time. Where was the court? Where were you your honor to hear me?

The system failed to protect me and to protect my rights, from dangerous, careless, incompetent, and negligent doctors.

The system has failed to protect me from being a baker.

The system has failed to protect me from hospitals and pharmaceutical companies that have failed me.

The system has failed to protect me from the violent and brutal representation of the law, sheriff, and Police, who had no consideration for a handicapped person and were not the last to beat me.

The system has failed to protect me from my father's wife Katherine's beating and bruises.

The system has failed to protect me from Carlos, a violent man, with a violent past in file.

The system failed when I was forced and court-ordered admitted to non-handicap-accessible State hospitals, behavioral facilities, and asylums.

I heard, from a social worker, of others who killed and have never been court-ordered to go to drugs, behavioral centers, or asylums. So why this treatment is only for me your honor?

I am claiming compensation for the health insurance company that never failed to pay during all these years without considering investigating my case.

I am claiming compensation for the Fifth Amendment not being respected, the lack of freedom, and the deprivation of the right to a fair trial.

I am offering a settlement.

My request is for reparation for all combined: I am claiming retribution and/or compensation for the Fifth Amendment not being respected, the lack of freedom, and a fair trial. For incompetency and negligence in the Hospital and for attempting to murder doctors, while admitted under a court order for drugs I was allergic to For eye drops in my food and overdose of drugs, the beating in hospitals, to pharmaceutical companies that used me as a guinea pig, the health Insurance company that failed to investigate my case over thirty years but kept paying, for being beaten, bruised in and out hospitals, by my relatives/family and their acquaintances while I was in a wheelchair and handicapped, and for being baker acted by the sheriffs and police and hospitals in general.

Copy is sent to the International Criminal Court for record and to some other people, press, relatives, congregation, lawyers, and some others overseas in which I have included all names, places with dates, facts of all events, attempting murders with names of people and places, etc... Just in case it would attempt to my life again. For information, I am aware of everything, names of legal people corrupted, their statutes, corruption, and names of corrupted persons...

Best regards,
Homicide

Later on, during that day and early afternoon, CHADD called me.

"VIE, I have a hernia and it does not look good. It is from Carlos beating me when my sternum was broken, and he bruised me a few months ago. Aggravated by the asylum-heavy wheelchair I am forced to use. Mine had been destroyed in the previous hospital when they brutalized me under the shower by the black pastor and I had a close head injury after a staff member dragged me backward violently and broke the anti-tip bars.

It is all red around the navel, it is swelling, and my belly button popped out. It does not look good, and I am in pain. The nurse was already concerned last night. I could not sleep, and I was in excruciating pain. She asked the Dr. to come and take a look at it early this morning. Dr. Li Kaos passed by me in the morning and said that he heard that I had to be checked by him. He never stopped though or gave me any examination. My belly button just explodes. He finally asked for an X-ray twelve hours later. Can you believe it?

This is not serious. I am waiting now with this pain in the belly. Then he hung up saying I got to go"
CHADD called me back later that day:

"I am back. I am such in pain they gave me some powerful narcotics. I am not feeling good. I am high and I do not like it. They did my X-rays and the nurse at the Bikenfreeze State Hospital commented that they should have brought me earlier this morning, now I will have to wait until tomorrow to get the results. Now I am going to lie down, or I am going to fall from the wheelchair. I'll call you when I wake up"
Then he hung up.

The next morning CHADD was still in pain, and it continued the entire day. Late afternoon Dr. Li Kaos came to tell him that he would put him on antibiotics the following morning, only.
He had the results but as he had narcotics early morning he could not give it before.

I felt the urge to communicate with Caroline and to leave a trace in writing.

"For fifteen days due to the ingestion of psychotropic drugs, he is becoming incompetent again, and at his last checkup, the nurse told him that he has developed a heart condition. All these people involved, keeping him on drugs, are killers. This is my opinion and I have the right to my opinion. I saved him years ago and got him back to a healthy human being and they are today making sure to keep him back in the same situation through drugs.

This is attempted murder.

I am the witness of a horrible homicide! But I will not only be an observer much longer.

Chapter 39
The Releasing Date

Finally, the date is approaching, and they are discussing his release, Archangel whose name means miraculous helper, tells VIE that they are considering a miserable and shocking amount for his compensation. That they were considering pittance. She is frustrated and finds that it is disrespectful. VIE decided to drop a mail to Carolina.

"Good morning Carolina, The compensation the system offers to CHADD is miserable and unacceptable. We are talking about compensation for the traumas he went through during the thirty-six years of his life and the deprivation of his rights. It's about the broken V amendments to the constitution that led to the degradation of his health because of the drugs that he was forced to ingest since he was in kinder garden, thanks to the infiltrated murderers thuggees doctors and while under court order to their care".

The system has failed him. The system has deprived him of protection from the Pakistani thuggees doctors, violence, poison, baker acts, rights, freedom, and a fair trial. A pittance for reparation and compensation is not acceptable, not even thinkable. There is no price for a life and to his life.

CHADD is offering a settlement for corruption of the system and attempted murders. He never killed, never assaulted, or brutalized anyone and he has been court-ordered twice to asylums for the same crime (that he never committed). Four hundred and eighty-nine days in "Chateau Asylum" and the second time where he is still in the "Beakimin Asylum".

CHADD has been brutally acted and arrested by two men in police "uniforms" The one that put the gun to CHADDS temple looked a lot like he was from Pakistan. One of them laughed at me when I said that I was a writer and taking note of everything. Well! Too bad Carolina because I have filed everything including names of MDs, nurses, and legalists that did not respect the law of the constitutions... and I mean names from top to bottom that have been part of this crime. I am aware of the entire corruption of the system, and of course, as I have no trust in justice I have taken my precautions.

I have sent copies of the file to various influential people in various key places in and outside the country with my authorization and instruction to be used if anything happens to CHADD or me.
Two days later, that was a Thursday, Carolina called VIE to inform them that he was going to be released on the first of the next month.

Five days later Dr. Li Kaos, in charge of the baker asylum, visited CHADD and let him know that his release was postponed for a couple of weeks for no medical reason. Now it was for the 17th.

Tuesday morning, which was seven days later, he had a review inside the hospital and was told that his release was suspended again.

The following morning CHADD called me to let me know that he had belly pain, his belly button out and looking inflamed the nurse asked Dr. Li Kaos to look at it as soon as he got in the morning. Li Kaos passed by him, and he heard him saying: "I heard that I have to check you" and he left without lifting an eye on him.

Twelve hours later, he felt his belly button exploding. He was told that he had a hernia and was rushed finally for X-rays to Freezem State Hospital. When he arrived the nurse in charge could not believe and commented: You should have been brought early this morning. Now you will have to wait until tomorrow for the results. This is not serious, and CHADD was left in sharp pain.

Mid-day, the next day, Dr. Li Kaos went to talk to him saying that he would start giving him some antibiotics but only "tomorrow" because he had already been taking psychotropic drugs and he could not mix them.

Too much is way too much, and I needed live traces and warnings before something bad could happen to CHADD. This hernia is the consequence of Carlos's beating and Carlos is free while CHADD's life could be in danger.

"Hi Carolina, I want to keep you posted on the progression of his case. He is in great pain, and I am warning that if anything happens to him I will press charges for murder, incompetency, negligence, and non-assistance to a person in danger. The Court is taking a great risk with his life, he should be moved into another hospital"

This phone call took me by surprise. It's 1:30 pm and my cell is ringing. I picked up and heard his voice.

"I was lying down; I was in such pain with the hernia, and they made me go to a class of anger management but all we do is play bingo. Vero the nurse came and pushed me out of the classroom to another room, where there was a man who introduced himself as Harry Soonor whom I had never seen before. Vero stayed, and there was another woman who introduced herself as my defense attorney. I told her that she was not my attorney, but Paul was his name, and I was not seeing him. VIE, you should have seen how fast I was moved out of the room, after that. But before they said that I going to be released earlier and it will be anytime from now and the end of the first week of the coming month"

The night before CHADD'S release he was called to take medications then a nurse pushed-ran him in his wheelchair in every hallway of the place. About fifteen minutes later he was finally wheeled into an office. CHADD felt very foggy and weird, his vision was blurry, and he could not think clearly. One man gave him some documents and told him "Sign here it is just a legal form that you must sign for your release tomorrow".

The release date, late morning, CHADD was wheeled in front of Harry Soonor. Harry Soonor's first phrase was "This meeting is illegal you have no public defendant or personal lawyer your release is postponed. You signed a conditional release form yesterday and that your case will be reviewed in a month from today"

Monday morning, I could talk to CHADD twice during the day but when I asked for the extension on

Monday night a man replied "Sorry mam, but that extension does not exist. That extension has never existed".

At the same time, I received a text from Carolina asking me to text her back immediately the name of the last judge that he saw and that postponed his release because she had to fax it quickly within five minutes to another authority in power. She said that they were depriving him of all rights and phone communications with me.

Chapter 40
An Alien Appeared To Us. Am I Sleeping Or Awake?

I am surrounded by energies from another planet.

We have been abducted and brought to another planet to preach, teach, and love other races of beings. I figured out to love on another level of consciousness and well-being where there is no poverty, no disease, no sickness, nothing. All is pure love.

When abducted everything I write is original. It's a new creation that began.

Good in the future? I am the chosen Aquarius that will affect the future. Freedom of thoughts, Ideas …. I look at the now and see how I can change that into the future.

Between 1984 and 2008 what was done by the Anunnaki was to classify and attack the state of the world today, and the state of the world in future Politicians and Government. They classified all Lightworkers for 24 years. The self-elected in key places governing this planet have classified, attacked, and put limitations on all the Lightworkers to be able to control you and your capabilities. You have been kept in slavery, poverty, and sickness with only a few DNA strands activated. It is time that you become your self-master.

Drugs, like marijuana open the aura to allow more attachment to come. They use anything that takes the body out of normal to make more attachments. Any drugs and alcohol do it. This is the biggest danger in the world and this is how they control people's actions. (Like pipelines) They create a pattern for people to kill themselves.

The Anunnaki wanted a one-world Government and began to attack the lightworkers because they could sense. They are being attacked the most. They have attachments in the heads of corporations, politicians, banks, courts, doctors, hospitals... everywhere.

It is the Illuminati, also called Archons and fallen ones that are doing all of this.

We are now more in the roam of evil than before.

They have created large concentration camp facilities already built with big fences, so no one can see the interior ready to hold a huge number of people.

They have railroad cars with shackles/ handcuffs built into the side of the car to transport in concentration camps. Transported standing up aligned handcuffed one next to the other. They have never enough power to fulfill them, and never enough money to fulfill them. They have provisions ready for them, and they are planning in the lab to release terrible diseases in the world and the USA, but won't release them until they have the antidote to protect them.

Chapter 41
Vision in a Dream of the Underground Action of the Illuminati

I am in a small plane, between four to or six seats only. I thought that one of the wings was going to hurt someone walking in the street. We are also on the Highway than on small urban streets, but finally, no one is ever hurt. Neither the people nor the wall of the houses. The pilot is very skilled.

Now, we are flying in a very low attitude between two mountains, between two trench lines and I am shown parked in shelters built inside big holes in the mountains big military tanks and trucks. We are not driving on the ground but we are flying in a very, very low altitude and the wings are so close to each side of the mountains that it is giving us the impression that we could at any minute touch either side. I do not see anyone inside the plane with me, nor the face of the pilot. I am only conscious of myself in the plane and of being an excellent pilot.

Chapter 42
Previous night vision

I am awakened, I know that I have to fight to avoid being attacked by the spirit energy that I am fighting.

I have to control my heartbeat and repeat to myself not to go into fear, not to open the matrix. I am feeling the wind, and I can hear it too. I am embracing a woman, now. I realize that it is CHADD's stepmother. It is Katherine. I have one knee on her breast to keep her on the ground. She has exorcised eyes. I can read that she is cared for one fraction of a second. She is suffocating, but still trying to possess me. I grabbed my VAJRA and in one quick gesture I swept her away once and for all.

Chapter 43
A quick Vision now

Four yellow papayas are ready to be picked but I am attracted by the three first ones.

I awaken and I was on the side of a little crick, where leisure boats are anchored.

The yard has just been cleaned with an enclosure and the next-door property is not, but there is a papaya tree with four sizes of fruits, yellow and ready to be taken. There are more fruits but they are still green. I am attracted to pick them up and more three than four because I thought I only saw 3 yellow though they are side by side. I think wild papayas ready to be picked up do not exist anymore. Of course, the papaya trees were planted by someone but the property did not belong to anyone and was left abandoned with wild bushes. I still feel that I want to pick up the four yellow papayas. The area has maintained a lot of its original vegetation and I cannot see any house. The leisure walk is pleasant along the water.

I did not see any buildings or any of the boats anchored.

Long and infinite discussion follows with my blue flame. Everything is Color-Light- Sound- Vibration.
It is time to awaken and to express Light by Love, to move to the next step, to what we are. The world egg symbolizes the sperm, the embryonic state of the cosmos, before its complete development. The world

egg contains all the possibilities of the manifestation at its potential state.

I am hearing that the whole project is a never-ending one as there is a continuation of energy and an infinite expanse of space to create from our universal mind. The world is our mind's creation, and we are moving in the direction of the Golden Age where compassion reigns and spiritual choices are simple and rewarding.

Union and nations are like rats and ineffective. It was nobody. Just someone who answered the phone call and said (I am Union Nations; I have his book and the cross. Stop calling here. But they are part of the plan for diseases. Dark energies. They started with good intentions and ...were attacked by the dark to serve their agenda.

As an Energy Retracting Transducer CHADD had over 1,000 attachments of dark energies (octopus). It was sucking him and had attachments by so many dark energies, so much that he could not be seen anymore.

The Archon's step-mother Katherine rematerialized and came with bad spirits inviting these bad persons to attach themselves to him. There are no good attachments. She has called them from all over the world. But I could not cut it off because it would have grown back. I had to freeze them in Light.

Lightworkers are also helping to suck it off with a spiritual vacuum cleaner. They not only removed it but they sealed it off the body so that no attachment can be reattached in the future using the oil essence of St Jude.

CHADD was seeing through my eyes, at that time, like adjusting his eyes through a telescope, through the attachments. Forty-eight hours later they worked on removing attachments on Policemen, judges, doctors...and removing them all from around him. They worked on his environment taking these people away and replacing them with good-hearted people. Workers, police, doctors, judges, all people that are going to have control over him in the asylum he was forcibly admitted.

He was saved from being poisoned by the dark energy & by Dr. Hernandez because and for the benefit, of the money they are making on him. Nurse Lauren Renson stole the anesthetic drugs used in surgery from Dr. ALSTER TANDOOHI (he has a British mother and an Indian Father) He is a Thuggee's descendant but came with good intentions, he just did not secure the medicine and she stole it. They used him. It is used in surgery in a very light dosage and has put him in a stupor state. She got all the information S.S., account number, etc... it all went back to the police, bank, doctors, and judge to protect themselves just in case he tried to defend himself.

Several people pre-plan for his food money. Katerine takes one hundred percent and divides it between Raimund, Macman the Manager at the 1-Ubank and a percentage also goes to Carlos, then Paul his brother also apart from the mother.

Chapter 44
A Chroma-Sonic New Planet

It is time for a new creation and a new beginning and we, CHADD and I have been abducted by aliens to go and Preach, Teach, and Love other races of beings.

CHADD is a Pisces, and he is coming from Planet Saturn. Saturn was a complex figure because of his multiple associations and long history. Saturn was the first God of the Capitol and was seen as a God of generation, dissolution, plenty, wealth, agriculture, periodic renewal, and liberation. In later developments, he came to be also a god of time. Saturn's reign was depicted as a Golden Age of plenty and peace. The Temple of Saturn in the Roman Forum housed the state treasury. Saturn the planet and Saturday are both named after the God.

VIE is an Aquarius from planet Venus that was once considered a twin to Earth. Venus was named after the Roman Goddess of Love and Beauty.

CHADD & VIE have to figure out how to teach Love on another level of consciousness and wellbeing, where there is no poverty, no diseases, no sicknesses but only pure Love.

The alien tells them to "Harsh quake and funky the planet". Spirit clear, mind setting clear.

The Chroma-Sonic Planet VIECH is inside an electronic storm. The interior surrounding of the vortex is Light and Sound, a Sonic Planet out of space (light and sound sonic planet)

There is gravity and the body dances with the Sonic Sound while the color changes with the music, it is a light vortex.

Teases and caresses explode with orgasmic, cosmic feelings releasing bubbles of colors. Many varieties of colors, and some are not yet seen by the human eye.

Very deep inside the mechanism of sexuality is a frequency. Sexuality is a frequency.

Freedom is available through sexuality frequency. Sexuality connects with a frequency of ecstasy, which connects back to the Divine source and information. That is also why sexuality should be taken seriously and only with a partner you care for. Rape is a rape for frequency.

Negativity concerning sexuality must be cleared. Sexual parts of the body are avenues to pleasure to be reinvented. Avenues of pleasure create frequencies that heal and stimulate the body and potentially lead it to its higher spiritual self.

Spiritual realms are places of existence that the human body is locked away from because sexuality was an opportunity for human beings to regain memory and reconnect with their spiritual selves and creator, or to find an avenue to the spiritual realm that is sealed off from us. The discovery of the highest frequency of sexuality arises from the love experience. When there are wars and killing, it engenders fears and phobias and keeps humanity through the Media, press releases, and TV away from freedom. Away from Love, away from sexuality, and the opportunity to regain memory and power. It is a way to keep you in slavery and to control, and deprive you of freedom. But you were born FREE.

I am hearing my blue flame; he tells me to write what is happening all around the planet.
All around the planet is Chaos. Humans are fighting for religious purposes. The chaos has been planted by the dark Government.

It is a fight of wars, against Ebola, implanted in mind of necessary vaccination shots, even offered free.

It is a war for control and money. The Thuggees are re-materialized, they have taken control of Psychiatry through pharmaceutical companies, mental hospitals, emergency walking centers, and doctors, and with the help of greedy beings in politics, justice, Government, and military … They have been introduced by a self-elected leader of the dark Government in power.

Do we need to appoint Nick Santana? No!
Who is he? One of them!!! They want to establish a third-world order Government. The control of the population.

We have to use the power of the good to stop the dark. Love is the answer.
The time has come that you become your self-master.

Chapter 45
The Real Power of the Words to Heal or Destroy

Words can bring life or death in this world and the next life.

The universe was created with a word. Words are not simply sounds; words have real power. The power to use words is a unique and powerful gift from God.

Words carry immeasurable significance. Jesus healed and cast out demons with a word. Christians have worshiped through words of song, confession, and preaching

Politics, education, business, and relationships center on words. It can destroy one's spirit, and stir up hatred and violence. Words can be used to help us reach our goals or to send us spiraling into a deep depression.

Of all the creatures on this planet, only man can communicate through the spoken word. But are the words used to build up people or destroy them, are they filled with hate or love? Are they filled with bitterness, blessing, compliments, love, defeat, or victory?

Words do more than carry information, they have the power to destroy and the power to build up. It can destroy one's spirit, create wounds, and stir up hatred and violence.

Jesus said, "But I tell you that men will have to give account on the Day of Judgment for every careless word they have spoken. For by your words, you will be acquitted, and by your words, you will be condemned"

Words are so important, that we are going to give an account of what we say when we stand before the Lord Jesus Christ.

Chapter 46
Five Days before Charlie's Attack

I headed to an office supply to buy an ink cartridge for my printer and some paper. I was comparing the different papers wanting to buy the best for the best price when I was taken by surprise, I heard someone asking me a question.

"Hello! I need to buy some too. Which one are you buying? I am interested to know which one you are buying and why you are choosing this one".

I looked at who was talking to me, and I saw a middle-aged Pakistani man. He is carrying some brochures and an Islamic 33-bead prayer, that he called "Misbaha" or "Tasbih" that he took out of his pocket while talking to me. Then he asked me to ask a question and said that he would pray on, with his Misbaha, and said that he would be able to answer my question. Then he continued the conversation, to which I was not paying much attention.

"You see, you are Christian, you have the Bible, the Jewish have the Torah and we Muslims have the Quran. The Bible has a piece, the Torah another piece, and we Muslims have the Quran which contains it all. Only the Quran is complete".

Then he began to explain that he was here to buy more paper because he was a writer, but he was poor and needed 1,000 dollars to go to New York to present his book. A book would make a difference in the world. To which I rapidly answered:

"Sorry, I am also a writer and unfortunately cannot help you with money'".

Good, said the guy from Pakistan, in that case, we should meet, we have to talk.

"Let us exchange names and contact information. You see there is a lot of confusion about Muslims and the Quran. There are different Branches and different kinds of Muslim communities. And I do not belong to the Muslim Mosque that belongs to Qatar. There is also the Illuminati with the entertainment industry, with Hollywood, with movies and music, and the dark Government with the politicians, the authorities in power, the oil companies, the pharmaceuticals, and it is all over the world. We should meet. You have nothing to worry about I am married, with grandkids."

All I wanted now was to pay for my paper and leave the place. I excused myself rapidly paid and left the place thinking, what was all that about? How did you find me? Why did the man approach me? What did he want from me?

Five days later the French news made the Media all over the world.

France was emerging from one of its worst security crises in decades after three days of attacks by gunmen brought bloodshed to the capital Paris and its surrounding areas. The gunmen identified themselves as belonging to the Islamic Terrorist group Al-Qaeda's branch in Yemen, which took responsibility for the attack. It began with a massacre at the offices of satirical magazine Charlie Hebdo on Wednesday, January 7, and ended with a huge police operation and two sieges two days later. The French Charlie's Hebdo magazine offices had been attacked and 12 people were killed in the attack on the Charlie's Hebdo offices. Eight journalists, two police officers, a caretaker, and a visitor. On January 11, about 2 million people, including more than 40 world leaders, met in Paris for a rally of national unity, and 3.7 million people joined demonstrations across France. The phrase Je suis Charlie (French for "I am Charlie") was a common slogan of support at the rallies and on social media.

Chapter 47
The Stigmata of Charlie

Why is the world hooked on Indigenous religions? Can't they see that it's all handmade? God is not a science. GOD is and always will be.

Chaos after Charlie's is chaos for Freedom and Christians are persecuted everywhere on the planet. From to millions of Iranian Christians, after the war, only three hundred thousand are left. Just because they were aspiring for Freedom!

Christian's persecution goes from verbal harassment to hostile feelings, attitudes, and actions. They pay a heavy price for their faith. Beatings, physical torture, confinement, isolation, rape, severe punishment, imprisonment, slavery, discrimination, and even death are just a few examples of the persecution they experience daily

Facing persecution by Isis, Christians in the Middle East, and the vitality of the Muslim world, the Vatican launched a Spiritual offensive.

All the chaos came from the Government, the elite, trying to scatter VIE and her work, trying to break VIE by draining her. They would love to see her let go of CHADD. But both are here to shed Light on the truth and found out themselves in a chaotic coucou land, with Isis and the Thuggees. The deceivers and killers.

So, I am asking you to go beyond, what the Government tells you that you should not go, and you will begin to see what you could not see before and open your mind. Because your mind is energy, and it has the power to transform and change matter that is only the physical manifestation of energy. Your awareness will bring the realization that causes an awakening that will bring you to enlightenment and you will find the truth, all the power is within you. It will then be a New Creation and a New Beginning.

Chapter 48
Restoration of Planet Earth

To restore Planet Earth, the repair begins in human consciousness. By caring for the land, the Earth, and the well-being of all human beings, present and future.

What did you come for if it is not to sustain harmony and balance of the Earth? What is life? Life is precious and if you want to survive you have to go back to the original, bring love and care for the planet. Love teaches you all. Love conquers all.

This is what you should work on by meditating on "I commit to the restoration of the Earth, to protect our land and water, to protect my brothers and sisters, and to protect our freedom"

All human beings have been created free and equal. By not caring for your brothers and sisters, by not caring for your planet, you are depriving yourselves of your birth rights and destroying the harmony and balance of the planet and the future of your children. You are all one in this adventure. You are all united and you are all involved in. Let the Love conquer, teach, repair, and restore for the good and the benefit of all of you. Do it now! It is time! Love will conquer all, you will finally remember, evolve, and grow.

Acknowledge that we are part of the symphony of the spheres.

The whole project is a never-ending one as there is a continuation of energy and an infinite expanse of space to create from our universal mind. The world is our mind's creation, and we are moving in the direction of the Golden Age where compassion reigns and spiritual choices are simple and rewarding.

As humanity awakens to the truth about our origins we can overcome our controlled and programmed slave nature and tap into our dormant DNA to realize and learn to make the difference between, the third world order and the creator's true loving God of the universe.

A little over two hundred thousand years ago some ancient Anunnaki astronauts were sent to Earth from planet Nibiru, in search of life-saving gold. They created the first humans as a slave race to mine gold. That started our global traditions of gold obsession. They used pieces of their DNA, controlling our capabilities and leaving us with only 3 % of active DNA.

The Anunnaki were using then, the power of Sound as a source of energy.

Mission words of the Lightworkers

That should be the world mission of all Lightworkers.

Chapter 49
Oat of the People in Light – The Mission of the Light Workers

"Pure in heart, pure in mind, pure in intent,
Though visions are manifesting
Though dreams are occurring
Though purposes in the world are fulfilling"

Chapter 50
OM (A.U.M)

Spiritual people are always talking about awakening, but what is awakening? It is simply awareness. You do not need books, gurus, cults, thuggees you don't need a bunch of bells and whistles to get there, all you need is awareness. With a greater awareness, and knowledge, of the body and mind it will naturally lead you to the awareness of the Soul. It's the unconsciousness of your mind that distracts from the Soul and with awareness, little by little, your mind will start to calm. It is not by fighting against the mind, not by struggle, but through simple awareness.

The worries and fears that thrived in unconsciousness start to shrink when it is exposed to the Light and is Cradled by the Sound Waves. OMmmm! OMmmm! Ommm! A vacation for the mind. In this, you will be transformed, and your feelings will become guideposts in how to live your life, not as an imitation of someone else, but as a celebration of your true self.

OM or AUM

A (transmit)

U (attract)

M is the motion that intertwines the combined thought of feeling aspect of consciousness.

Human beings, everything is encoded in your DNA. Your original DNA consisted of 12 active strands of genetic material. The ascension process to the 5th dimension involves the reconnection of reassembling your DNA strands that have been disconnected, and the activation of your 22 strands of DNA.

Many technologies are available that will open the DNA up to 12 strands, but it requires the service of one who carries the spiritual authority to do this work. For 24 years, the self-elected in key places governing this planet (all these dark energies that control the planet and create genocides, through drugs, plant diseases, poverty, pollution, and wars) have classified, attacked, and put on the limit all Lightworkers to be able to control you and your capabilities. Keeping you in slavery, poverty, and sickness with only a few DNA strands activated. It is time that you become your own Master.

We are moving from 3rd-dimensional consciousness into the prophesied 5th Golden Age of Light, peace, and prosperity. Anyone seeking to be a conscious part of this transformation will begin to manifest themselves, their lives, and their work at a new higher level.

Chapter 51
And the Time Came for Divine Intervention

The father told VIE, in a very upset tone "I have sent Mother Theresa to take care of the poor, sick, and the dying in Calcutta. Communicate and work with Mother Theresa. The VAJRA is still in Calcutta they want to use it during their next pagan celebration cult. This is the time to disclose everything"

These Thuggees are born in that life with a good level of intelligence that they use against the American people. They are the ones that have been cast out of India and now it has a tight link with all the US Indian/Pakistani doctors in general and mostly, Psychiatry – Psychology and Scientific doctors, Scientists. Also, Pharmacists, pharmaceutical companies, nurses, States, and private hospitals … have sneaked into the United States and made their way slowly inside the country. They tried to release a disease, but they already lost. They failed with Ebola, and they failed because the medical field had a way to stop it.

These dark forces that were working to destroy and control in the past have worked under the great veil of secrecy. Without anybody knowing what they were doing.

They are the Indian and Pakistan thuggees reincarnated. They are called the "deceivers" They are here to kill people in hospitals, with drugs, and to refrain American citizens from freedom. The VAJRA will be recovered disintegrated and rematerialized into your possession between today and the New Year. I will guide you to use it when the time will come. Expect it back soon, very soon."

That same night I saw God sitting at the judge's place in Court. Justice had the number 33 for the face.

I knew that it was confirming my intuition.

The phone rang and a woman named Candy Chapel asked to see me. I gave her an appointment for the following Tuesday early afternoon.

When Candy approached me I felt a sweet and calm energy and when she introduced herself to me her voice was very calm and warm. She did not have much to say but she wanted to hear as much as she could, I told her that we were a Duo, but CHADD had been baker and kept on Psychiatric drugs for 5 years for no medical reason and that my office had been vandalized with all the furniture taken. I also told her that I noticed that a Nano camera had been installed in the ceiling and that the day I discovered that I had been vandalized I went straight to address the camera saying: You do not know who I am so leave me alone, then 15 days later all furniture was back and reinstalled.

I saw Candy concerned for me and even nearly fear in her eyes as she said:

"Are you sure that you are safe now in this new office? Do you feel comfortable and safe here? When she was reassured Candy Chapel left after firmly hugging me and whispered to my ears "Thank you for doing what you are doing"

Three days later I received the answer from my Guide.

"Candy Chapel had a sweet, calm, and peaceful energy because she was sent to privately make an investigation on some illegal activity by the Court and on some people that elected themselves in Key places inside the court that are handling CHADD case and to see who you were. She was investigating the breach of the Fifth Amendment. She had nothing against you. She needed to see what type of personality you have and what you knew that could help her investigation.

The other woman named Gabriella who came to visit you directly from her visitation in India was searching for information about it, but she came first, and you did not have anything to say anyway. She was sent by the Thuggees and the third world order."

One-week later CHADD called me and from the tone of his voice, I could understand that something happened that disturbed him.

"VIE, I received a phone call from Paul, he was blaming you for all that his mother Katherine did to me for 35 years. He is trying to protect her by making you responsible for what she did. He said that you admitted me 78 times in facilities and signed me out also and then he placed Katherine on the phone. I hung up but she called back. As I greeted her with my usual Pastor CHADD speaking, Katherine began yelling at me, saying that I was not a Pastor neither a Minister or any Reverend and she gave me a long and agitated speech with so many lies about you that I had to cut the phone communication again. I could not stand to hear all these lies. I do not understand why they want me to sign my release from this Bakerinn State Hospital. I have been admitted without a fair trial but a farce. Who then signed me in, if Paul and Katherine pretend they can get me out for the holidays and what type of power do they have in Court if the court admitted me in? What type of power do they have to play court hearings inside mental hospitals? I knew something was going to come up when this morning, at the Bakerinn State Hospital they asked me to sign some legal papers that I refused to.

Are they trying to make me cover up something or legalize some illegal papers? I have a weird intuition on this one, I think they have put themselves in an illegal and fraudulent situation and now they want you to be blamed for it. What is going on now?

Since I have been here Caroline never called me, but I know that she spoke to the social worker this social worker is not a very truthful person and it seems that it is all about money.

You know I am considering asking my dad to take me off his insurance policy. Let us see what they will do then if the hospital is not getting paid. Will my monthly Government check cover the hospital bill? I don't think so.

One-night Paolito the gifted healer, who lives in Santo and works guided by Sainte Rita, was awakened by her. She instructed Him to go and visit Maria in Cebu.

Sainte Rita: Paolito you must go and recover the VAJRA; a diamond ring is attached to it. It is very important. Go Maria Tranh-Kruger-Pile pile will know she is expecting you. She recovered it from an Asian couple from Calcutta. They stole it to VIE to do some Pagan ritual with it.

Finally, the VAJRA reappeared in my possession. The VAJRA was disintegrated first and then rematerialized.

My Angels cleaned all the attached dark energies off the VAJRA and ring.

The stolen diamond ring from the office was recovered from the South where it was sent, was not used then passed to someone else and came back to me attached around the recovered VAJRA chain.

All my other stolen jewelry was disintegrated to prevent anyone from using my energy.

The VIETCH was auctioned by the Thuggees doctors in the South which was illegal as it was still CHADD 'S title and responsibility, and they kept the money.

We CHADD and VIE, are the Spiritual Warriors chosen by GOD. We are an old cosmic couple in human form. We have been created to battle an invisible battle for the Souls of the Highest Government of the Universe.

We are fighting the battle for CHRIST.

God's Key Holders
Time Travelers

Chapter 52
To Those Who Control and Misapply Justice

I sat to meditate, and I received a message from my friend the encountered "medium whales". He told me that the heart and soul of the planet Dolphin are part of the great feminine divine, sister of Gaia, alive and here. Planet Dolphin is a mirror for your soul, in this 3D universe and the land carries now the gold spark of the unseen fire of God"

My message to you is that peace will be on Earth and awakening will happen. It is a consciousness of many billions stirring souls alive and growing, and it will not stop. It cannot be stopped.

To those who cause fear and to those who manipulate, choose peace now. Peace is the thing that your soul has searched for in your deepest. Choose peace when the moment comes and when you have a choice. It is the moment. Do not fire a gun, do not add chemicals, and do not press that key. Just be brave and choose peace.

Here is my call to you for Justice:

You, who have placed yourself in key places for control and power, surrender, surrender yourself and the power to His Love. The time has a chance. The Light has filled the dark, turn yourself to the Light. The invisible light that permeates the air that you breathe will not stop. The end is near, the end is here, and it is inevitably His law, His Light, His justice that wins. Stop controlling, stop killing, stop abusing, stop stealing because you are still yourself, stop restraining, and stop misapplying justice.

One God, One land of Freedom under God, and justice is for all.

Light cannot be subdued or controlled. Light cannot be manipulated or owned, for Light is freedom and I am His Light.

Commanders of forces, commanders of armies, men and women in positions of power, religious authorities, men of Law, in Courts and Justice, doctors, reporters, film producers and entertainment industries, actors, and bankers you are incarnated humans, you are men and women of Mother Earth that loves you. Be brave choose peace. When you take off your outfit, your uniforms at the end of the day look at your body and look at who you truly are. Think about the future of your children.   Think well. Choose for the benefit and well-being of all. We are all one.

Look at the world you live in, look at the water and skies you polluted, and see the reality of truth and love and Light. It is surrounding you, it is everywhere, in the air that you breathe and in all that you do. Be courageous, be brave, and choose peace.

The invisible unseen fire of god is here, and it will not stop. Beware of the doG.

May you be blessed by your infinite Light.

In Love and Light always."

Is it fact or fiction?

VIE BIO:

In January 1987 VIE experienced a dramatic shift in consciousness resulting in a complete change of lifestyle. During her first contact experience, VIE's galactic mission and purpose were revealed and gifts from previous interplanetary incarnations were activated. She is a visionary, vibrational transformation, and metaphysical Healer and clairsentient. Books author and musician. VIE speaks the language of the Light that she also sings, songs, and chants, and she carries the authority to activate your 22 DNA, raise your energy, erase your stuck emotions, and feel to ease your pain.

VIE is the creator of 'Bio-Qi Therapy TM", and the owner/founder of the Institute of Biostimulation (DOB) also the Institute of Light & Sound. She gives sessions on one in her office or in Quantum.